# NONVIOLENT
# POWER

# NONVIOLENT POWER

## Active and Passive Resistance in America

Judith Stiehm
*University of Southern California*

**D. C. HEATH AND COMPANY**
Lexington, Massachusetts   Toronto   London

This book is dedicated to E. Richard Stiehm, Eleanor Hicks, Carmen Gil de Leon, Vimal Singh, Verity Berg, Doris Chu, Margaret Blanford, Grace Healy, and Montez Ewing. I am grateful for the assistance and criticism of Haskell Fain, Jane Hadley, Ken Dolbeare, Christian Bay, and Paul Hare.

# Contents

Introduction                                                                ix

### 1 American Nonviolent Resistance                                         1
Two Cases of Nonviolent Resistance                                           1
A Selective History of Nonviolent Resistance in America                      3
Summary                                                                     18

### 2 Nonviolent Resistance: Terms and Types                                19
Terms Used in the Literature on Nonviolent Resistance                       19
Types of Nonviolent Resistance                                              25

### 3 Individual Nonviolent Resistance                                      34
Assumptions of Individual Nonviolent Resistance                             35
Aims of Nonviolent Action                                                   38
The Power of Individual Nonviolent Resistance                               41
Techniques of Individual Nonviolent Resistance                             44
Mass Individual Nonviolent Resistance                                       52
Applied Individual Nonviolent Resistance                                    54
Conclusion                                                                  58

### 4 Group Nonviolent Resistance                                           60
Assumptions of Group Nonviolent Resistance                                  60
Power and Consent                                                           64
Components of Group Nonviolent Resistance                                   68
Hierarchy and Nonviolent Power                                              71
Techniques of Group Nonviolent Resistance                                   76
Applied Group Nonviolent Resistance                                         79
Conclusion                                                                  81

5    **Combined and Contrasting Explanations of Nonviolent Resistance**    85

The Christian View of Nonviolent Resistance    85
Proportional Nonviolent Resistance    88
Combined Explanations of Nonviolent Resistance    92
Contrasting Explanations of Nonviolent Resistance    97

6    **Social Change and Nonviolent Power**    103
Philosopher-Kings and the Sovereign People    103
Democracy and Nonviolent Resistance    105
Problems of Nonviolent Resistance    108
Criticisms of Nonviolent Resistance    111
Conclusion    113

**Epilogue**    117

**Selected Bibliography**    118

**Index**    129

# Introduction

In the early 1960s American social reformers discovered (or rediscovered) nonviolent resistance. In particular, civil rights supporters committed themselves to this method of social change, and their numerous and varied activities culminated in the "Freedom Summer" of 1964.[1] Today those recent events are thought of as history. Enthusiasm for nonviolent resistance has waned even if it has not entirely withered away, and political rhetoric now rings with cries of "violence" and "revolution" rather than with appeals to "nonviolence" and "resistance."

Why? Why have so many Americans, including some of the most effective practitioners of nonviolent resistance, forsaken so promising a method? The answer, in part, is probably that while nonviolent resisters had high expectations, they lacked useful explanations. Their actions were more often based on the imitation of past success than on a clear understanding of nonviolent resistance and its mechanisms. This meant that techniques were indiscriminately transferred from one situation to another. Further, those resisters who did have some philosophical understanding of nonviolent resistance, who could define it, explain it, and outline its limitations, frequently were dismayed to find their beliefs incompatible with those held by their allies and supporters. This made collective action difficult to sustain. It also made coherent communication with opponents, with observers, and with potential supporters improbable if not impossible.

If the civil rights activists of the early 1960s had understood nonviolent resistance better, if they had recognized that there are at least two quite different kinds of nonviolent resistance and that they are based on different premises, lead to different conclusions, and are suited to different situations, then they might have used it more selectively, more successfully, and more perseveringly. In addition, others who seek social change might have found nonviolent resistance a more attractive weapon.

The first kind of nonviolent resistance is based on the assumption that all men have a potential for good. Its activities are directed toward communicating with others or arousing their consciences. It works through persuasion, which requires contact with one's foe, and it seeks reconciliation. All concerned come to agreement; they share both their goals and their priorities.

The second kind of nonviolent resistance seeks to avoid the destruction

---

[1] There are a number of interesting accounts of this venture. Some are Sally Belfarge, *Freedom Summer* (New York: Viking Press, 1965); Elizabeth Sutherland, ed., *Letters from Mississippi* (New York: McGraw-Hill Book Co., 1965); Nicholas Von Hoffman, *Mississippi Notebook* (New York: David White Co., 1964); and Howard Zinn, *SNCC, The New Abolitionists* (Boston: Beacon Press, 1964).

let loose when men use violence. Its goal is to establish alternative ways of settling conflict, ways that are less costly than violence and that may well involve coercion. This form of nonviolence emphasizes strengthening the resisters' commitment, cohesion, and number. Its goal is a redistribution or reorganization of social power. It does not aim at harmony.

Each of these views of nonviolent resistance includes a set of assumptions and a group of conclusions. Unfortunately, the tenets of each view are logically incompatible even though they exist together everywhere. What then is the reasonable advocate of nonviolence to do? The best course may be to follow the example of the physicists who have learned to live and deal effectively with two contrasting theories of light, one of which describes it as continuous waves while the other refers to it as discrete particles. Thus, two different explanations are put forth, accepted, and used alternatively. They are not confused. They supplement but do not interfere with each other.

In the past, those who have successfully practiced nonviolent resistance have usually used the two kinds together. Those who have simply glossed over the differences or who have focused on only one type have tended to fall into disarray when confronted with failure. Those with a resilient approach have usually seen nonviolent resistance and society itself in a broader frame. To be specific, they have recognized that society is composed of an elite with many resources and of a mass where individuals have few resources. They have seen that the elite acts with special intelligence and initiative but that the mass can veto any decision it vigorously opposes. Those who pursue change have to see society with at least this degree of complexity. They must perceive that different methods of change will be workable in different situations and for different groups.

Both explanations of nonviolent resistance assume that power has two components—right and might. The first explanation offers a Platonic vision of right as a "real" truth that is potentially perceivable by all although it is currently unperceived by most. The second adopts a more pragmatic view of truth as that which the largest number of concerned and committed persons believe to be true.

Although an advocate of the first theory may hold that anyone can become a philosopher-king, that is, see the truth, an activist will especially wish to demonstrate his truth to those who hold power. This is because they can most easily command change. If the activist's truth is at odds with the interests of those who hold power, he may do better to focus on the second theory and to concentrate on developing a veto by the people. The crucial limitation of this approach, which is based on the "sovereignty" of the people, is that it can only veto; it cannot initiate. It can dispose but it cannot propose. In any society, only a few define what is right; their might can be described as intellectual. Still, the mass must always acclaim the right; their might, then, is numerical.

Those who hold power at any particular time are usually enthusiastic about having others limit themselves to nonviolent kinds of action. Those out of power frequently find this hypocritical. They see, and sometimes feel, the legal and institutionalized violence extant in any society. But nonviolent resistance should not be underestimated, either as to its potency as an agent of change or as to the costs it will exact from a resister. It can persuade elites to make top-down change; it can also mobilize the people to refuse specific social policies. Sometimes this happens without cost, but more often it is at great cost.

It is important to remember that nonviolent resistance is expensive. Persuasion frequently requires extraordinary creativity and ingenuity, and pressure demands long-term commitment, special organizing skills, and readiness to sacrifice. Furthermore, while change is always costly, in nonviolent change most of the costs are borne by the agents of change. Indeed, these persons are often denied even the pleasure of feeling efficacious. This is because authorities frequently deny that a resister's acts in any way influenced later change. The authorities are unwilling to admit (often even to themselves) that they have responded to pressure, or as they describe it, to blackmail. The costs of nonviolent action are different from those of violent action in other ways too. First, the resister risks death instead of threatening it; second, the leader goes to jail rather than the follower; and third, success is measured by what the resister actually gains and not by what he costs his opponent.

Indeed, the hard fact is that nonviolent resistance is so costly that few readers of this book will ever practice it. Like the author, they are probably too comfortable and too privileged to be likely participants in or leaders of a mass movement. On the other hand, even though they may rub shoulders with the individually powerful, few readers are among them. Because they do not feel individually effective, they will not be likely to practice individual nonviolent resistance. Still, if nonviolent resistance is practiced, the readers may well play a crucial role. Even if they think of themselves as "uninvolved," they may serve as the "impartial observers" who morally judge others' individual acts of nonviolent resistance; or they may, as agents of the state, be directly challenged by the acts of group resisters and have to decide to repress or not to repress—literally, to shoot or not to shoot. In concert with others, then, they may affect the course of history even though none of their names are ever noted. Though they neither direct nor defy society's power, they may, in fact, determine how it is used.

# 1  American Nonviolent Resistance

## Two Cases of Nonviolent Resistance

Today auto emissions are a political issue. A little more than a decade ago, not even atomic emissions were of much concern to most of the American public. Both Russia and the United States freely tested nuclear weapons and each scattered their radioactive debris on the winds of the world. But in 1957 a group of thirty citizens organized to put an end to such testing. Committed to the proposition that our country's "defensive" activities could lead only to the destruction of what we sought to defend, this group sought to demonstrate its belief through action. Sure of their perceived "truth," the members of the Committee for Non-Violent Action Against Nuclear Weapons (CNVA) set out to persuade American leaders, and if necessary, the American people as a whole that bomb testing was unconscionable and unreasonable. Their answer to the question "But what can a man do?" was, in essence, "One can act dramatically and symbolically to bring out the good resident in all men."

One CNVA act involved "swimming in" at the launching of a Polaris submarine. Another act involved sailing a 30-foot ketch from San Pedro, California, to the 50,000 square miles of the South Pacific that had been designated as a nuclear testing area. The hope was that the presence there of four U.S. citizens would cause U.S. officials to reconsider and eventually halt their tests; if it did not, it was hoped that the protesters' martyrdom would cause the American people to force the officials to put an end to such testing. The members of CNVA chose to challenge their government by risking their lives. They sought to effect change by offering themselves as a sacrifice. Accordingly, four middle-aged, middle-class men set their sails to the wind in February of 1958.

Their journey was not serene. Within two weeks of their departure the sailors found themselves back in California, the victims of illness and inclement weather. Their second voyage was more auspicious, and their ship, the *Golden Rule*, made it to Hawaii without incident. There they notified Navy officials of their plans and there the confrontation with the U.S. government began and also ended. During this contest, the crew of the *Golden Rule* continually sought to show the immorality of the government's behavior, while the government attempted to demonstrate the ordinary illegality of the sailors' behavior.

For instance, an inspection of the *Golden Rule* was made by the Army when the ship first arrived in Hawaii and another was made by the Navy after it tried to sail on. It was found that the identifying letters were not parallel with the waterline and that one of them was one-eighth of an inch too short. Further, the government issued an executive order making the trip illegal *after* the first part of the voyage (from California to Hawaii) had begun.[1] Finally, the government sought and received an injunction forbidding the trip. Thus, simply by setting sail (as they soon did) the crew would become liable to charges of contempt of court and of conspiracy.[2]

After the sailing, arrest, and conviction, concerted negotiation began. The government first offered the resisters a suspended sentence and probation in return for their agreement to help "rehabilitate themselves" and to refrain from breaking any laws in the future. The *Golden Rule*'s crew refused to pledge their future behavior, however, even though they did not have any specific plans. Indeed, even after they were finally released (on probation and with suspended sentences), the crew spent three weeks trying to decide whether or not morality dictated that they engage in further illegal action. All were gravely concerned about the implications of breaking criminal laws concerning contempt and conspiracy. On the other hand, CNVA members and supporters who were conducting demonstrations and civil disobedience on the mainland were anxious for the trip to proceed. They strongly urged action and eventually the ship did set forth again; this time it was stopped six miles out at sea, allegedly under the rules of "hot pursuit." Again the crew members were arrested and convicted. This time they were jailed for sixty days. By the time they were released, the case and the trip were moot. However, the *Golden Rule*'s mission was actually accomplished by another dissenting sailor, Earle Reynolds, who did sail into the forbidden area and who witnessed an atomic explosion before he too was legally harassed with an arrest and a conviction. An appeals court finally reversed his conviction two years and many dollars later. Meanwhile, the Committee for Nonviolent Action continued its acts of witness and its offerings of personal sacrifice in a variety of ways and in a variety of places. Ultimately the United States and Russia did sign a nuclear test ban treaty. That was in 1963; today nuclear fallout is no longer a part of our everyday air pollution problem.[3]

In May 1971, 30,000 young people calling themselves the Mayday Tribe gathered in Washington, D.C., and called for an end to the Vietnam War. With the sanction of a government permit they camped along the banks of the Potomac River and enjoyed rock music, sex, and drugs, and cavorted publicly in the nude. Acting according to plan and with some coordination, they stalled traffic, blocked bridges, let air out of tires, and rolled garbage cans in the streets. About 5,000 police, 1,500 National Guardsmen, and 10,000 federal troops were deployed for the event. In less than two days officials made more than ten thousand arrests,

---

[1] The order was canceled five months later.

[2] Any protester would be well advised to study closely federal and state laws governing conspiracy. One can be convicted of this felony if one agrees to commit any illegal act, even a misdemeanor, if any party to the agreement commits any overt act to further the plan. Thus, even if no illegal act is ever done, and even if one takes no action at all himself, he can be convicted of a serious crime.

[3] Albert Bigelow and Reynolds have described their contests with the government. See Albert Bigelow, *The Voyage of the Golden Rule* (Garden City, N.Y.: Doubleday & Co., 1959) and Earle Reynolds, *The Forbidden Voyage* (New York: D. McKay Co., 1961).

lodging their captives in outdoor detention centers, in army tents, and in a football practice field. Tear gas permeated the capital for a day; and within two days most of the arrested had forfeited $10 as collateral and returned home. The war they were protesting continued and no government official condoned their behavior. Still, both legislative and executive branches made strong moves toward ending the war after this event.[4]

What is the relationship between these protests and subsequent events? Surely one of the most frustrating tasks facing the nonviolent resister is to establish a cause-effect relationship between his resistance and subsequent events or decisions. The relationship between the acts of the *Golden Rule*'s crew and those of the Mayday Tribe is also hard to establish. What elements do the two demonstrations have in common? How are they similar? Further, are these unorthodox, political acts of witness or of protest new or are they old? Is nonviolent protest only a mid-twentieth century phenomenon in the United States or has it been advocated and practiced throughout our history? Does the evidence show that nonviolent resistance originated with Rosa Parks's weary refusal to yield her bus seat in Montgomery, Alabama, in 1955, or does it suggest that nonviolent protest has had either a continuous or a continuing tradition, or both, in this country, and that it has manifested itself in many different kinds of activity? Does history link the phenomenon to only certain times and places or does it suggest that it is bound to neither time nor space and that analysis of it is therefore of value? In each of these pairs of questions it is the second portion that seems to make the better case.

## A Selective History of Nonviolent Resistance in America

### The Beginning

The history of nonviolent resistance in this country seems to date at least from the New England Quakers' firm insistence that they be admitted to otherwise well-regulated Calvinist enclaves, and perhaps it should be dated to the apocryphal tale of the rescue of John Smith by the Indian princess Pocahontas who died in 1617 in England as the wife of another John but who physically obstructed the bashing out of Smith's brains.

The Quakers' insistence on taking up residence in Calvinist towns involved a commitment to the acting out of the principles they held. It involved the taking of direct action by individuals (or by small groups) who believed they had the right and even the duty to live as and where they chose regardless of the opposition or obstacles encountered. Pocahontas's act, in contrast, involved the spontaneous use of her last resource—her physical presence. While hers was also an individual act, probably it was unpremeditated, aimed at a particular goal, Smith's rescue, rather than at the embodying of a principle, and rooted in passion,

---

[4] The U.S. Senate voted total U.S. withdrawal within nine months if U.S. POWs were returned, and the President announced that he planned to visit Peking within the year in order to promote peace.

not conscience. From the beginning, then, nonviolent resistance has sometimes been rooted in strong and consistent conviction, and sometimes in sheer desperation.

In the first set of circumstances the resister is usually consciously and permanently committed to the practice of nonviolence. He tries to practice his conviction himself; more importantly, he deliberately transmits his belief from one generation to the next. In this way a tradition is established that lends legitimacy to later individual actors. This continuous tradition of nonviolent resistance is usually practiced by single individuals or by groups acting in parallel or with unanimity. In contrast, in the second set of circumstances nonviolent sacrifice or offer to sacrifice occurs more or less spontaneously; that is, it is produced by the pressure of events. This kind of nonviolent activity may be individual, as it was in the case of Pocahontas, but often it is collective. Because of the periodicity of its recurrence, this kind of action yields what can be described as a continuing tradition of nonviolent resistance. As it becomes more frequent, effective, and widespread, however, the likelihood that it will be consciously imitated, organized, examined, and even preplanned increases. Indeed, the year 1955 may represent a landmark in the history of nonviolent resistance, for it may be that since that time genuinely spontaneous or situation-produced nonviolent resistance has no longer been possible. Since then, the possibility of organized, collective nonviolent resistance may have become so much a part of American thinking that it can no longer simply "happen." Certainly one explanation of nonviolent resistance can best be described as an attempt to express rationally and to mobilize consciously what has previously been experienced as a natural, unconscious, and amateur kind of collective action. If analyses of this sort become widely enough known and accepted, collective nonviolent resistance will, like individual nonviolent resistance, become a continuous rather than only a continuing strand in American political thought and action.

Generally, it was Christian and not secular nonviolent resistance that was practiced in pre-Constitutional America. The story of the Quaker, William Penn, his excellent relations with the Indians, and his Pennsylvania "Experiment in Government," has been told many times.[5] A more unhappy and less well-known story from that same period concerns the nonviolent resistance practiced by a group of Indians converted by Moravian missionaries. Their acceptance of Christianity and of nonviolent principles was apparently so complete and so effective that they passively submitted to mass slaughter by their fellow Christians —westward-aspiring American settlers.[6]

During the Revolutionary War advocacy of nonviolence was not in style, but interestingly enough, the Boston Tea Party, in which settlers dressed

---

[5] For further exposition of the Quaker position and of Penn's "Experiment," see Staughton Lynd, ed., *Nonviolence in America: A Documentary History* (New York: Bobbs-Merrill Co., The American Heritage Series, 1966), pt. 1; Isaac Sharpless, "Colonial Pennsylvania: The Quest for Non-violence," in *The Quiet Battle,* ed. Mulford Q. Sibley (Garden City, N.Y.: Anchor Books, Doubleday & Co., 1963), pp. 210–30; and Peter Brock, *Pacifism in the United States: From the Colonial Era to the First World War* (Princeton, N.J.: Princeton University Press, 1968), pp. 81–132.

[6] Recounted in William Miller, *Nonviolence* (New York: Schocken Books, 1966), pp. 224–29.

in Indian garb and threw boxes and boxes of English tea into the salty Atlantic, is cited again and again as an example of nonviolent resistance. This is done even though that celebration involved concealed identities, clandestine activity, and the destruction of property—all three of which are factors that violate most definitions of nonviolent resistance.

The unpopularity of the War of 1812 coincided with the formation of a number of peace societies dedicated to nonviolence. This kind of organized protest was a new phenomenon, and one that was to continue through the 1830s and indeed right up to the Civil War. All through this period, peace organizations tended to concern themselves with the problem of slavery as well as the problem of war; their concern, then, became dual.

## The Civil War and After

It may be quite natural to suppose that in periods of relative quiet a commitment to nonviolence is an appropriate and normal accompaniment of a commitment to peace, to justice, or to some other fine cause. It frequently becomes evident, however, that in periods of crisis one's different commitments are not necessarily compatible. Advocates of peace frequently conclude that a "genuine," or lasting, peace is possible only when certain conditions have been met, and that those conditions can best be attained by war. Similarly, persons who are devoted to a particular version of justice often find themselves presented with an apparent opportunity to win their goal if they will but temporarily resort to the violent means that they have previously renounced.

William Lloyd Garrison is an excellent example of a man who found that his beliefs in peace, in nonviolence, and in emancipation could not be permanently harmonized. In the pre–Civil War era, Garrison was probably the best-known of the abolitionist-pacifists; he was the author both of the manifesto of the American Anti-Slavery Society (1833) and of the declaration of the New England Non-Resistance Society (1838). In the latter Garrison wrote, "We recognize but one King and Lawgiver, one Judge and Ruler of Mankind (God)," and "We expect to prevail through the foolishness of preaching—striving to commend ourselves unto every man's conscience." In this period Garrison totally disavowed even the use of the political process, including the electoral process. At the same time, he preached, he argued, and he urged a wide variety of nonviolent action and resistance.

Once the Civil War broke out, Garrison and his fellow abolitionist-pacifists were confronted with a dilemma. Their goal, which was emancipation, and their preferred means, which was nonviolent resistance, seemed to be in conflict. Confronted with this situation, many of them chose to relinquish their method rather than their end, and therefore they lent support to the Northern cause. Garrison's own change was dramatic and complete: his support for the war became fervent and he joyfully proclaimed it the best possible way of "exorcising" the South of its "deadliest curse."[7]

Because of this change of heart, Garrison is not usually enshrined in

---

[7] Lynd, *Nonviolence in America*, pp. xxiii–xxx, 25–31.

the annals of the nonviolent, and perhaps he has not had a direct influence on current thought about nonviolent resistance. It could have been indirect, however. Today's students of nonviolence almost inevitably drink long at the springs of Gandhi's thought. Ghandi in turn credited his own inspiration to three sources— the New Testament, John Ruskin, and especially Leo Tolstoy. To complete the circle, Tolstoy asserted that it was William Lloyd Garrison who first proclaimed the principle of nonresistance to evil as the basic principle for the organization of man's life.[8] Thus, the doctrine of nonviolence might be said to have been on a one-hundred-year leave of absence from the United States. During that period it visited both in Europe (Tolstoy's Russia) and Asia (Gandhi's India); now it has returned home only to be confronted with many of the same problems as those that confronted Garrison. Injustice continues and the society remains racially divided. In the interval, though, changes have occurred and thought about non-violent resistance has greatly increased in sophistication.

Americans have fully enjoyed the fictional works of Leo Tolstoy, but his works on pacifism, which advocate the literal interpretation and acting out of New Testament injunctions, have been less widely circulated. Perhaps the reason these works are not often read is that they are both highly religious and highly perfectionist in tone. For instance, Tolstoy avers that any compulsion whatsoever, be it ever so habitual, or be it no more than the simple possession of more goods than the average, is a form of violence. It was also his view, however, that at bottom people are the "oppressors of themselves" because they submit to demands that they could reject. For instance, they report when they are called to military service instead of staying home or leaving the country. Tolstoy's general perfectionism may find a sympathetic audience among individuals who are separately committed to the practice of nonviolent resistance. His second point, however, has particular meaning for those who are interested in group resistance. However, the tone of today's group organizers is much more secular and much more pragmatic than Tolstoy's was.[9]

Another nineteenth-century American author who attracted the attention and won the respect of Tolstoy was Adin Ballou. Ballou's essay "Non-Resistance in Relation to Human Governments" was published in 1839; his utopian community, Hopewell, was founded in 1841 and endured until 1856. Like Tolstoy and many of those who practice nonviolence individually, Ballou based his thought on Christian texts and pledged his devotion to an anarchism that rejected any participation in government or any "revenge at law." On the other hand, his essay reflects the thought of present-day group resisters because it emphasizes the power and the efficacy of nonresistance.[10]

---

[8] Ibid., xv. See also Leo Tolstoy, *The Kingdom of God Is Within You* (New York: Noonday Press, 1961), pp. 7–12.

[9] Tolstoy's most significant works on the subject are *Letter to a Hindu* (London: Peace News, 1963); *The Kingdom of God Is Within You* (New York: Noonday Press, 1961); and *The Law of Violence and the Law of Love* (London: Westminster Press, 1959). See especially *The Kingdom of God*, pp. 181, 297. See also chaps. vii and xii.

[10] Adin Ballou, *Non-Resistance* (Boston: Non-Resistance Society, 1839).

It has already been noted that when the Civil War began, many abolitionists abandoned their pacifism. Some, like Garrison, went directly to wholehearted support of the "just" war; others, like Wendell Phillips, first passed through an intermediary stage in which they justified self-defense. Still others, however, maintained their commitment to nonviolent resistance. War violated their principles even more than the existence of slavery did. Most Quakers and Mennonites held firm; Ballou remained steadfast; so did the members of the League of Universal Brotherhood, which had been founded in 1846 by Elihu Burritt, a highly self-educated blacksmith whose organization had its origin in the "54-40 or fight" crisis, in which the United States and Great Britain contested the control of Oregon.

Burritt's league was a precursor of the next century's nonviolent civil rights movement. He himself made explicit the reason for having an organization. It was to enable individuals to do more than conduct protest in parallel; it was to impart new strength to protest and action by making it collective. Burritt even urged that collective activity take such modern and coercive forms as the general strike. While the governing principle of his organization was called passive resistance, it was a resistance that gave conscious consideration to the group, and to such concepts as power and economy. Among the many group activities conducted by Burritt's league were peace congresses and ladies' sewing circles, and the amassing of pacifist pledges—some 20,000 of them.

Groups devoted to nonviolence and peace enjoyed a revival following the Civil War. At that time, the American Peace Society, which during the crunch had held that it was necessary to "crush rebellion" with "police powers," again began to increase its membership and it was joined in its purposes by the newly founded Universal Peace Union. The latter organization had as its president from 1866 until 1913 a gentleman appropriately named Love. This group was based on the proposition that peace could not endure unless it was grounded in justice. Thus, it concerned itself with the creation of just social arrangements. In particular, it promoted the civil rights of blacks, women, Indians, immigrants, and even labor. Concern for the last group was especially modern; for as one scholar has noted, peace advocates have historically manifested a remarkable "blindness to economic factors."[11] Again, these advocates of nonviolence were committed to two goals—peace and justice; again, these goals seemed mutually compatible; again, there was no necessary relationship between them. In addition to these formally declared peace organizations, native (as contrasted with immigrant) anarchists like Josiah Warren worked to further the tradition of nonviolent resistance. So did a large number of social reformers like Jane Addams, Clarence Darrow, and William Jennings Bryan, all of whom, at one time or another, made pilgrimages to Tolstoy's farm community in Russia.

Between the Spanish-American War and World War I, college students, as they periodically do, lamented the lack of causes to which they might

11 Merle Curti, *Peace or War* (New York: W. W. Norton & Co., 1936), p. 134. Much of the narrative in this chapter is drawn from this excellent book.

dedicate themselves, and peace became a noncontroversial topic of conversation and of discussion. Business, church, and educational institutions all commended it; Andrew Carnegie funded a foundation to promote it; President William Howard Taft asserted that questions involving national honor ought to be submitted to international judicial processes rather than to a contest of arms; and President Woodrow Wilson went so far as to appoint a pacifist, William Jennings Bryan, as secretary of state. Wilson himself ran for office on the slogan "He kept us out of war." The world seemed to be at equilibrium.

### World War I

With the start of World War I, the peace movement in Europe "crumpled like a house of cards";[12] it sustained severe damage in the U.S. also. Once more, advocates of peace and justice had to decide whether peaceful or warlike conduct was the most certain way to win their various goals. Miss Addams chose peace and went to work on Henry Ford and Rosika Schwinner's proposal for a Peace Ship; she also became the first president of the Women's International League for Peace and Freedom. Mr. Bryan resigned from the cabinet. Mr. Darrow, on the other hand, chose to limit his dislike and disavowal of violence to conflicts that were domestic in nature. Similarly, the Carnegie Endowment declared that there could be no peace until Germany was defeated, and it acted to cut off all funds for European peace groups. The American Peace Society displayed its feeling, as it had during the Civil War, that *American* was a more important part of its title than *Peace* was—or else it believed that the way to win peace was by war—and quickly rallied to the war effort. Indeed, it rallied so quickly that it began to support the war before it was declared![13] At the same time a number of new organizations concerned with nonviolence were formed, and it should be emphasized that this occurred during and not after the war.[14] Also, new techniques for nonviolent action were devised about this time. From this we may make two observations. First, preferred ends and the preferred means for obtaining them are not always compatible. Justice and peace do not always go together nor do freedom and majoritarian democracy. One must sometimes choose one or the other; one must be able to establish priorities. Second and more important, it may be that conclusions about the strength and focus of people's commitments can only be drawn under conditions in which difficult choices must be made, when either ends or means must be chosen, or when one end must be chosen over another.

---

12 Ibid., p. 229.
13 Ibid., p. 254. As this volume clearly shows, peacetime pacifism is not an unusual phenomenon.
14 All during the war a number of clergymen steadfastly maintained their opposition to the military, and to violence. Among these were John Haynes Holmes, Norman Thomas, and A. J. Muste. These individuals and others with similar beliefs were among the founders of the Fellowship of Reconciliation (FOR), organized in England in 1914 and in the United States in 1915. This group has provided advocates of nonviolence and social justice with an effectively functioning organization from that day to this. It has also fostered a number of specialized groups to deal with particular social problems; the best known of these ancillary organizations are the American Civil Liberties Union (ACLU) and the Congress of Racial Equality (CORE).

World War I brought to the American male a new legal obligation—military service. It thus created a new kind of criminal—the draft refuser. It is true that conscription had been practiced fifty years earlier during the Civil War. However, in the North one had had the option of hiring a substitute, and in the South one could win exemption by paying a bounty. Both escape routes were closed during World War I, and those persons who would not serve in the military suddenly became visible and vulnerable. The strength of their belief was put to a severe test, for World War I legislation was even less generous in the exemptions it granted on the grounds of conscience than later selective service acts were. At that time the only claim for such an exemption was one derived from the doctrine of a "well-recognized" religion. Even then, the objector was not exempted from military service—he was exempted only from combat duty. Altogether, 2,800,000 men were called to service in World War I. There were 64,000 claims of conscientious objection, of which 56,000 were allowed. Nevertheless, 4,000 young men refused to cooperate with the military in any way. The final disposition of this recalcitrant group was as follows: 1,300 ultimately agreed to serve in a noncombat role, 1,200 were furloughed, 100 were permitted to work for the Quakers in a service capacity, 900 were being held at the time of the armistice, and 500 were court-martialed. Of those convicted, 64 were sentenced to 25 years or more in prison, 142 to life imprisonment, and 17 to death! Happily no executions for draft resistance occurred.[15]

An interesting psychological and sociological study of America's first resisters to the draft was made following the war.[16] The resisters were found to fall into three more or less distinct categories: religious literalists, religious idealists, and socialists. The first two categories were found to represent a cultural phenomenon—men assigned to them were described as being the conforming product of particular subcultures. The motivation of the third group was thought to be more amenable to psychological than to sociological explanation. The only empirical generalizations arrived at though were that the nonviolent socialists (1) had a highly individualistic life style, and (2) had higher IQs than other draftees. The conclusion, then, was that there are two types of individual nonviolent resisters: one conforming to a religious subculture; the other, political and deviant. Both groups, however, were composed of persons committed to a set of principles for which they were willing to sacrifice. Collective pragmatic resistance was not studied or considered in this investigation. Perhaps it could not be clearly perceived until after the suffragette and labor struggles of the 1920s and 1930s.

## Suffragettes and Workers

New groups put nonviolent resistance to more aggressive and more political use following the war. For example, the suffragettes elected to pursue their cause outside ordinary political channels. In particular, they favored the two

---

15 See Mulford Sibley and Philip E. Jacob, *Conscription of Conscience* (Ithaca; Cornell University Press, 1952), pp. 12–14.
16 Clarence C. Case, *Non-Violent Coercion* (New York: Century Co., 1923), chap. 11.

techniques of mass picketing and sustained picketing. They also offered voluntary suffering through civil disobedience. To do this, they broke laws. If arrested and convicted, they served jail sentences instead of paying fines. Once jailed, they fasted—sometimes so completely and for so long a period of time that a further form of suffering, forced feeding, was entailed.

Other social reformers concentrated on the woes of labor. Real gains were made during the quarter century between World Wars I and II; what is more, they were made without class war, civil war, or other organized and sustained violence. The interesting thing about this is that while the labor movement seems to be an excellent model of successful group nonviolent action, its struggle was not advertised as nonviolent, nor is it usually classified that way. The crucial question is whether labor's success was achieved because it did *not* renounce the possibility of using violence (it did make its potential for violence clearly evident); whether its success was due to the nonviolent techniques that were actually, if unconsciously, employed; or whether its success was due to other circumstances entirely.

Why weren't the struggles of the labor movement perceived as non-violent? The most important reason is that the movement's leaders did not so proclaim it. It is probably also significant that the struggle was chiefly between two private parties. This meant that because neither had a legitimate claim to the use of force, neither could very appropriately renounce it. Further, the strategy of each side involved enlisting the government as its ally, and although the government in its third-party role of arbiter, judge, policeman, lawmaker, and/or negotiator does act coercively, it is usually thought of as acting legally (or illegally) rather than nonviolently or violently. This is because governmental power is expressed through law—an entity that for most is symbolically associated with the dignified trappings of the legislative chamber and the courtroom, although for others it is associated with the billy club and prison bars. Still another reason for not referring to the labor movement as nonviolent is that its goals were so immediate and so clear that attention was focused almost exclusively on them— on the ends desired. Little time was available for the investigation and proclamation of the philosophical and ethical implications of the means chosen to achieve them.

The rigors of labor's struggle in the 1930s were so severe that they caused a number of professed pacifists to overcome their scruples concerning the use of violent means to combat injustice. Among these were A. J. Muste and Reinhold Niebuhr. Muste was a Presbyterian minister who had been forced to give up his church because of his pacifist opposition to World War I. In spite of this earlier sacrifice, Muste changed his mind. He was so deeply affected by the cause of labor that he concluded that the workingman's suffering could not adequately be ministered to by a person committed to nonviolence. Therefore, during the era of his "labor ministry" Muste forsook pacifism; he became a Trotskyite. Eventually, however, he recommitted himself to Christianity and redirected his energies first toward the problem of civil rights, and later toward the problem of peace-making through direct nonviolent action.

Niebuhr, a Lutheran minister and once national chairman of the Fellowship of Reconciliation, experienced a similar falling away from pacifism when confronted with the realities of the labor versus Ford struggle in Detroit, where he had obtained a pastorate soon after completing his theological training. In *Moral Man and Immoral Society,* Niebuhr argued the occasional necessity of using coercion and even violence to win justice. In the same book he also argued the case for the situational use of nonviolent resistance. He urged in particular that the American black explore and utilize that form of resistance, not for ethical reasons but for pragmatic ones: blacks are in the minority.

The 1930s produced two collective nonviolent action techniques that were to reappear in the 1960s in other contexts. The first was the "sit-in" strike, which was first used in the auto industry in 1936–37. This device served the worker in two ways: first, it inconvenienced the employer by withdrawing cooperation; and secondly, it prevented him from acquiring cooperation from another source. In sum, production was stopped and overhead costs continued. The second technique, that of marching on Washington and camping out there, was pioneered by the Bonus Army in 1932. (Dispersal of such armies was pioneered by U.S. Army officers Douglas MacArthur and Dwight Eisenhower.) Both these techniques were intended to be nonviolent, although both were also intended to be coercive by being threatening. Admittedly neither tactic could easily be executed altogether without violence, and so both were roundly condemned by most of the day's opinion leaders.

It can be said, then, that in this period "passive resistance," a primarily individual activity with an ethical concern as its foundation, gave way to— or perhaps more accurately, was joined by—"nonviolent resistance." The latter often involved collective and aggressive behavior and was directed toward achieving particular and worldly goals. Coercion was its very purpose, not its pariah. Still, even though the two varieties of nonviolence were contemporaneous they were not often linked together. Probably it was the struggle waged by Gandhi in India that finally brought U.S. social reformers to the realization that perhaps individual, moral, passive resistance could be efficacious, and that strictly pragmatic group nonviolent resistance might be made more successful if full publicity were given to the moral soundness of its tactics.

## After World War II

It was after World War II that American advocates of nonviolent resistance first began consciously to merge these two views—to think of nonviolence as both expressive and instrumental, as both ethical and pragmatic, as both passive and aggressive, and as both individual and collective. The leaders of this new trend were men who had themselves undergone a variety of experiences in their long-term personal efforts to further social justice. Many of them had worked in the labor movement in the 1930s, maintained a pacifist position throughout World War II, and turned their attention to civil rights and peace after the war. These men included Muste, James Peck, David Dellinger, and Bayard Rustin.

While academics began analysis and discussion of this new phenomenon in such magazines as the *Journal of Conflict Resolution,* the men mentioned here founded their own journal, *Liberation,* which has served an important contemporary function in maintaining communication between the various peace and civil rights organizations and between the theorists and practitioners of both individual and collective nonviolent resistance.

Although overlapping memberships do create substantial linkage, modern peace groups and civil rights groups have tended to remain distinct. Further, although both types of organizations frequently are nonviolent in behavior, neither type necessarily adheres to a doctrine of nonviolent resistance. Indeed, some of the peace groups are definitely not adherents of the philosophy of nonviolence. For example, SANE, which has had as one of its moving spirits Norman Cousins of the *Saturday Review,* is specifically not unilateralist or universalist; it is nationally oriented, and (under pressure from the former and late Senator Thomas Dodd of Connecticut) it purged Communists from its membership rolls. Other groups like Turn Toward Peace gathered together so large a combination of groups that it was difficult to discern just what, if any, principles were held in common; and still others so highly valued spontaneity and decentralization that they, too, were virtually without agreed-upon principles. Dagmar Wilson's Women Strike for Peace represents this type of organization.

Many of the members of these groups were "nuclear pacifists," people who argued only that no one could profit from nuclear war. Their purpose was preventive and they especially thrived while the U.S. was not deeply involved in war. When the Vietnam War escalated, new antiwar groups came into being. Many of these were temporary coalitions; few of them were committed to a philosophy of nonviolent resistance; their members were opposed to the Vietnam War, not to war in general. On the other hand, most of these groups were nonviolent in practice because their leaders believed, probably with good reason, that this was necessary if wide support were to be developed. Although the antiwar movement has apparently not created any lasting organizations, it has been effective. In 1968, 62 per cent of the U.S. population favored a fight to the end. By 1971, only 36 per cent favored this.[17]

Nevertheless, peace groups that are clearly pacifist in orientation have remained numerous. Those first organized at the time of World War I include FOR, the American Friends Service Committee, and the Central Committee for Conscientious Objectors. The Catholic Worker Movement was born during the depression. World War II products included the War Resisters League, and cold war groups included Peacemakers, which has emphasized nonpayment of taxes as its form of resistance, the Student Peace Union, and the Committee for Nonviolent Action.

Peace groups that advocate nonviolent activity have a certain advantage over those that focus on creating the "necessary conditions" for peace, whether those conditions are world government, exchange of hostages, or Esperanto. The

[17] Richard Rovere, "Letter from Washington," *New Yorker,* July 17, 1971, pp. 70–75.

advantage is that they can, at once and unilaterally, begin to practice what they preach. Their action is not dependent on anyone else's action. Believing it wrong to fight, they have only to refuse to fight. Their principles can be carried out immediately and directly, with or without ado. They can make their position the status quo position. This is an enormous advantage. It is the same kind of advantage that in the field of civil rights sitting in at a lunch counter has over something like voter registration. The resister can take the initiative and do what he believes must be done. He can only be prevented from doing it by strenuous action on the part of his opponent. In short, in some forms of nonviolent action, the advocate of change is able to take the initiative; when he can, he gains important leverage.

The other main cause with which nonviolent resistance has been recently associated, and the field in which it has probably been most visible and most approved is civil rights. In this area the resister usually has a specific goal in mind. Nonviolent action is not thought of as an end but as a means to the accomplishment of a particular purpose or set of purposes. Unfortunately, many civil rights goals cannot be unilaterally accomplished. Cooperation of others and response from others are required. For example, voter registration requires the cooperation of a county clerk; home purchase requires agreement from a home owner, a real estate agent, and a banker; a high-status job requires affirmative action on the part of an employer and perhaps on the part of a union. Thus, careful calculation as to what techniques will change prejudiced attitudes or discriminatory behavior becomes imperative. One-sided action simply does not suffice.

Since World War II the most active civil rights groups have been the National Association for the Advancement of Colored People (NAACP), the Urban League, the Congress of Racial Equality (CORE), the Southern Christian Leadership Conference (SCLC) and the Student Nonviolent Coordinating Committee (SNCC). With the possible exception of SNCC, which has officially become SCC, none of these groups has advocated or used violence to promote its cause. The first two organizations (founded in 1910 and 1912 respectively) have never really engaged in a debate about the use of violent or nonviolent resistance. In the purest sense, neither of them could be called nonviolent because their activities are often very coercive—they involve lawmaking and law enforcement. Also, in the most normal sense, neither can be called nonviolent; this is because they are so committed to working within the system, they have never found it necessary to renounce violence. One does not renounce what one does not contemplate.

CORE was founded as an offshoot of FOR in 1943. Although its members need not be pacifists, its past leaders and most of its activities have been in accord with that philosophical position. James Farmer, the first and longtime national chairman of CORE, was a participant in the 1947 "Journey of Reconciliation," which was essentially a dry run for the 1961 "Freedom Rides" that made CORE famous. In contrast to SCLC, CORE is urban and northern. It is also a group that has undergone a number of rapid changes. Its changing attitude toward the limiting of nonviolent activity to noncoercive activity has been well documented in Farmer's book, *Freedom—When?* Its changes in leadership and in style are analyzed in Inge Bell's *CORE and the Strategy of Nonviolence*.[18]

The two remaining civil rights groups consciously adopted and advocated a policy of nonviolent resistance at their inception; both were and are chiefly black and southern in membership. SCLC was founded in 1957 as an outgrowth of the Montgomery bus strike, and SNCC was founded in 1960 with the support of SCLC to encourage southern college students in their sit-in activities. The Reverend Martin Luther King., Jr., was the central leader of both organizations during their infancy. Prior to his work with these groups, however, King was not a philosophical advocate of nonviolent resistance. In his very interesting essay "Pilgrimage to Nonviolence," King recounts the way that he came to this belief, and it is made quite evident that his belief was as much a result of successful action as it was of meditation.

Histories of the postwar civil rights movement are readily available from a variety of sources, and the events are familiar to most Americans. The Montgomery bus boycott of 1955 is usually thought of as its beginning and this perception is probably as accurate as any, but a number of trials or "experiments" that were run in the 1940s ought to be recalled because they suggest, once again, that techniques have to be applied in the right circumstances to be effective. Although a number of these trials "succeeded," the techniques were not transferred to other situations, perhaps because there were not enough professional or youthful risk-takers available, or perhaps because the public was not yet addicted to the TV news.

James Peck and Bayard Rustin were among the CORE members who first utilized the restaurant sit-in. That was at Stoner's in Chicago in 1942. The same men also participated in the Journey of Reconciliation, mentioned previously, which tested the integration of interstate bus service in 1947. The bus companies failed the test, but CORE also failed to effect a change at that time. Peck also participated in other campaigns, including an attempt to secure admission of blacks to the Palisades Amusement Park in New Jersey (1948) and service at dime store lunch counters in St. Louis, Missouri (1949).

After the Montgomery bus struggle, the next significant events of the civil rights movement were the student sit-ins. These began in 1958 when the NAACP Youth Council in Oklahoma City found itself engaged in such action; but the 1960 sit-ins that erupted all across the country were sparked by college students in Greensboro, North Carolina. Perhaps the most important outcome of these protests was the formation of SNCC.

The interaction of the various civil rights groups in these sit-ins should make it clear that the competition and conflict sometimes apparent are often due not to philosophical divergence but to personal or other immediate factors affecting particular situations. That this is so is shown by what happened at Greensboro. The demonstrations there essentially erupted—they were unplanned. Once

---

[18] James Farmer, *Freedom—When?* (New York: Random House, 1965; and Inge Powell Bell, *CORE and the Strategy of Nonviolence* (New York: Random House, 1968).

they began, the students sought counsel and went to a local NAACP officer for advice. Instead of contacting his organization's main office, he called in a CORE representative who immediately began training the students in the techniques of nonviolent resistance. SCLC also responded, and King himself came to Greensboro to lend his presence to the cause. Last, but not least, an NAACP youth director lent his services to the students.[19] Each organization responded and contributed what it had to offer in that particular place at that particular time; philosophical differences did not affect cooperative action and were not even identified or necessarily perceived as existing.

The organized use of the economic boycott, which has sometimes ensnarled rights efforts in laws prohibiting secondary boycotts, also began in the 1960s. That such a device could be effective in southern towns, where blacks represent a high percentage of the buying public and where they can boycott all items sold by all merchants of a community, is easily understandable. However, the device was also used to good advantage in northern cities. In Philadelphia, for example, selective buying campaigns that focused on the products of single companies said to discriminate in their hiring practices were pursued. This was done even though secondary boycotts were against Pennsylvania law and no formal organization could be acknowledged. The boycott was accomplished, nevertheless; ministers throughout the city, who had apparently formed their plans out of the blue, began announcing to their congregations on Sunday mornings that they personally had given up purchasing particular products.

A few attempts to create across-the-board changes in a single community's racial practices through nonviolent resistance were also made. The campaign in Albany, Georgia, met almost total defeat. In part this was because a wise police commissioner responded to nonviolent resistance with equally nonviolent and apparently routine law enforcement. In contrast civil rights efforts in Birmingham, Alabama, were more successful. This was partly owing to lessons learned by the resisters at Albany; they were better prepared. It was also, however, partly owing to almost unrestrained law enforcement, which included the unleashing of police dogs on schoolchildren. The resisters were assisted also by the individuals, never apprehended, who blew up a church during church school classes murdering four children, and by the fact that industrial Birmingham had northern connections that were embarrassed by the treatment of the resisters. The then secretary of defense, Robert MacNamara, for instance, made a number of concerned telephone calls to the executive officers of Birmingham's chief steel producers. The lesson of Birmingham, as both sides noted, was that for repression to be successful it must both remove the possibility of a counterresponse, and also not provoke third parties into intervening on behalf of the oppressed.

The year 1963 featured a march on Washington, a demonstration in which Asa Phillip Randolph played a main role as he had done in a series of less famous marches in 1956 (20,000 participants), 1958 (8,000), and 1959

19 Louis Lomax, *The Negro Revolt* (New York: New American Library, Signet Books, 1964), pp. 134–36.

(25,000).[20] While the other marches had been smaller, part of the reason for their failure to capture the imagination of the public was the total lack of governmental, especially presidential, response. Such a response was not lacking in 1963, however. President John Kennedy met with march leaders, congratulated them on the dignity and fervor of their demonstration, and promised to battle for sweeping civil rights legislation. Also in 1963, rent strikes were organized in New York City and school boycotts were held in Boston and Chicago. The arsenal of nonviolent techniques grew and grew.

The civil rights movement of the 1960s peaked with the Mississippi Freedom Summer of 1964. This featured the mysterious disappearance and murder of three civil rights workers. Two of them were white New Yorkers; the third was James Chaney, a black Mississippian. Subsequently, northern civil rights supporters tried to help right this dreadful wrong by bringing north Chaney's younger brother, Benjamin, and providing him with the best our liberal culture has to offer. The wrong was not rightable. In the spring of 1971, Benjamin Chaney was involved in the wanton murder of several whites. Angela Davis, who was tried for the murder of a white judge in San Rafael, California, was a church school classmate of the girls murdered in the Birmingham bombing. Whites as well as blacks suffer from the backlash phenomenon.

Tension and activity remained high throughout the summer of 1964. In the fall, the civil rights movement carried its struggle to the national convention of the Democratic party. There a slate of Mississippi Freedom Democratic party candidates presented its credentials, and there they wrested more concessions from a principal party than any other black group had.

Throughout this period much of the nonviolent resistance was neither individual nor idealistic. It was collective, coercive, and goal-oriented. Since that time, NAACP and the Urban League have continued their activity in their traditional ways; they have emphasized law, persuasion, and self-improvement. The newer organizations, SNCC, SCLC, and CORE, however, have experienced increasing criticism, decreasing financial support, and internal conflict. Some have attributed this to their intrusion into the area of Northern human relations problems such as de facto segregation of schools and housing. Others blame their decline on their linkage of civil rights and anti-Vietnam War activity. It is significant, however, that the success of much of what SNCC, SCLC, and CORE did in their heyday was accomplished by the simplest of means, means which required only modest and short-term financing, activity, and commitment. The 1964 Freedom Summer, for instance, required only a summer commitment by college students, most of whom were without dependents and without a need to work.

To continue their success, civil rights organizations will have to devise new tactics to meet more complex and less visible problems. They will have to attack vested interests and they must expect to be attacked in return. They will have to challenge old and revered institutions, not just those that are defended

---

[20] Randolph had also participated in the planning of a march as early as 1941. This was cancelled when President Franklin D. Roosevelt agreed to create the Fair Employment Practices Commission.

with a certain amount of embarrassment and guilt. Most important, they will have to examine themselves.

Those who seek change will have to examine their goals and priorities. They will have to construct their alliances for maximum effect both as to breadth of membership and as to depth of conviction and length of commitment. They will have to recognize that radicalism is not a lark—that it is most often practiced by those with nothing to lose and that those who do have something to lose should engage in radicalism only if they are prepared to make sacrifices. (College students usually have a great deal to lose.) Even if civil rights workers do decide to assume real risks they must not expect that those with nothing to risk will fully trust them. They won't, and they are right not to. It was Mayor Hubert Humphrey, from a moderate-sized midwestern city with few black residents, who fought a glorious civil rights battle at the Democratic National Convention in 1948. It was Senator Hubert Humphrey, however, with a vice-presidency to lose who "settled," that is, quieted, the civil rights challenge made at the 1964 convention.

The point is that nonviolent resistance has not "failed." It has simply won the obvious and easy victories. Any number of delicate and difficult tasks remain. Before they can be properly tackled, however, a careful reassessment of goals, resources, and techniques must occur. The civil rights warriors of 1964 were dismayed to find they were not an army but only allies—and tenuous ones at that. Many of the white activists were able to repress the collapse of the civil rights movement by channeling their energies into antiwar activity.[21] Perhaps the scale of Vietnam's horrors made such a change in the direction of their efforts appropriate. Still, it was an easy route to take, because it quickly became evident that Americans were regularly killing noncombatants, that their technological warfare was indiscriminate warfare, that higher taxes would be required to pay for the slaughter, and that middle-class and upper-class boys would be drafted and sometimes killed. In short, antiwar activity quickly became not only a "moral" but a very "self-interested" activity. The true mettle of the antiwar movement will be tested only when the war becomes what has been called manageable—that is, when it has been reduced in scale until only a limited number of people have a direct interest in its end. This will occur when American casualties are few, even though our country may be routinely bombing any number of other countries and their people. The critical point will occur, too, when employment is full and inflation is controlled, even though an excessive portion of our production may consist of war material. It is then that we will learn how committed the antiwar protesters are, and how well they understand the techniques of protest—how well they can select their target, martial their resources, and sustain their effort.

Movements pursuing social change can succumb either to excessive cost or to the excessive complexity of a problem. They can also succumb either because too few people have an obvious stake in the change or because the stakes they have are too different. The last point is important because in general our

---

21 The Gulf of Tonkin incident occurred in August 1964. Regular bombing of North Vietnam began in early 1965. Thus, the escalation of the war coincided exactly with the ebbing of the civil rights movement.

government bases its action on what it calls a consensus. A consensus is a very limited kind of agreement. It is an agreement *to* a decision or *to* an action. That is, the agreement is only to an outcome and not to the justification of the outcome. This means that a particular policy can be supported for a wide variety of reasons—some or many of which may be contradictory. Thus, opposition to a particular war could be based on the belief that it is insufficiently profitable, or on the belief that it fattens the purse of only large corporations. Opposition could be based on one's desire to stay alive, or on one's wish to spare the lives of others. It could be rooted in one's support for Communism or in one's desire to fight the "real" war—a nuclear one against a major rather than a minor power. The point is that those who support or consent to the status quo or to official policy rarely have to discuss their reasons. They do not have to reveal any misalliances that may exist. In contrast, those who seek change, or those who oppose the government, must continually explain. In doing so, they reveal their disunity not only to their opponents but also to themselves. Thus, if change based on consensus is to occur, sophisticated alliances have to be built. Otherwise change must await obvious and overwhelming self-interest or unanimous and spontaneous altruism. Both are rare phenomena.

## Summary

There has been a continuous tradition of individual pacifist thought and practice in this country since its inception. In addition, formal peace organizations have been organized at regular intervals, and there has been a periodic recurrence of nonviolent mass movements. Some of these movements have later turned to violence (as abolitionism did), while others have focused on a single issue and died with it (suffrage for women). Still others have essentially practiced but not conciously adhered to nonviolent resistance (the labor movement). In recent years there has been a merger of two different kinds of nonviolent resistance in both the civil rights and antiwar movements, a merger of the individual, principled type and the collective, goal-oriented type. This has been accompanied by a shift in the vocabulary used from terms like *pacifism* and *nonresistance,* to *nonviolent resistance.*

In the United States today, the theorists of nonviolent resistance usually are not the same individuals as the activists. Men like A. J. Muste, James Peck, and Martin Luther King, Jr., were or have been so involved in their work that they have lacked the opportunity to analyze. They have not thought carefully and systematically and then spelled out for others their assumptions and the implications of their assumptions. Still, some individuals have tried to explain nonviolent resistance systematically, and have endeavored to relate it to experience. They include Richard Gregg, who has approached nonviolence as primarily a problem in individual morality and psychology; Gene Sharp, who perceives it as an effective tool for promoting the goals of minorities and of unarmed majorities; and Harvey Seifert and William Miller, who have attempted to combine these two perspectives and also to reconcile them with the traditional Christian view of violence and nonviolence.

# 2  Nonviolent Resistance: Terms and Types

Most present-day literature on nonviolent resistance is either exhortative or descriptive. It seeks to incite, to persuade, or to record; only rarely does it attempt to analyze. Because precision is not often a primary goal, one finds in the literature on nonviolent resistance that definitions are frequently left unclear and distinctions obscure; premises are not well articulated and conclusions are not logically drawn. Clarification, therefore, requires first that fairly precise definitions be established for the terms most frequently used, and second, that the distinctions used in establishing different types of nonviolent resistance be carefully outlined. Only then can the assumptions and implications of the various explanations of how nonviolence works be satisfactorily examined.

## Terms Used in the Literature on Nonviolent Resistance

The key word requiring explanation is *nonviolent*. By virtue of its prefix this term would seem to have as its equal and opposite, *violent*. One might then expect that he could solve the problem of definition by defining either of the two terms and asserting that the second is the antonym of the first. Unfortunately, such polar definitions do not satisfactorily encompass the whole. The two words are not contraries.

While it seems clear that a physical assault must be characterized as violent, and while it seems equally clear that to ask quietly in private, "Are you sure that is a wise thing to do?" is not violent even if it is not nonviolent, it is not at all clear how one should classify such activities as economic boycotts, which threaten the livelihood of others, or sit-ins, which may snarl the flow of freeway traffic or prevent others from enjoying recreational or educational facilities. Probably the latter acts are best described as "coercive," and probably it is through this concept that one must approach a definition of *violent* and *nonviolent*.[1]

When one acts coercively one attempts to alter another's behavior without necessarily changing his beliefs or attitudes. One attempts to manipulate

[1] The attitudes of American males toward violence are explored in "Attitudes Toward Violence," Monica D. Blumenthal, Robert L. Kahn and Frank M. Andrews (paper prepared at Survey Research Center of the University of Michigan, 1971). One interesting finding is that illegal behavior is considered more violent than legal behavior and behavior of disliked individuals is seen as more violent than that of liked individuals.

another's behavior by altering the external circumstances that influence his choice. Coercion, then, involves the changing of the environment. It means the creation of new options.

Usually coercion is accomplished by attaching one or more penalties to actions one finds deplorable, so that alternatives will appear desirable. Logically, however, coercion can also involve the attachment of rewards to alternatives one wishes to promote.[2] Still, in practice, the "carrot" technique is not usually felt to be coercive or described as such. Even though temptation may have the same effect as threat and even though it may involve similar ethical issues, it simply does not affect people in the same way. For this reason coercion, violence, and nonviolence are commonly associated with negative sanctions only—with those alterations in environment that penalize an individual who acts in an undesired way.

Those attempts to change the behavior of others that are appropriately called noncoercive seek to change an individual's attitudes or convictions rather than his options. The ultimate goal may be to change social circumstances, but the immediate goal is to change how circumstances are perceived. Any number of dramatic devices have been and are employed to provoke new perceptions and responses; some of these techniques will be discussed later. At present, the question that must be answered is how coercion and noncoercion relate to violence and nonviolence.

Some advocates of nonviolence maintain that to use coercion in any amount or of any kind is to use violence. They argue that to create any physical or mental discomfort whatsoever is to act both violently and wrongly. A logical but hardly sensible conclusion that can be drawn from this line of reasoning is that one must avoid any act that would so much as embarrass one's opponent, even if the act involves no more than the publication of facts previously concealed by him.

Other theorists of nonviolent resistance, especially Christian theorists, assert that the definition of violence is not tied to the physical nature of the act but is related to the "spirit" with which it is performed. Thus, one can say that any act done "in love" is nonviolent no matter how gruesome it may seem, while any act done with malice may be violent even if no physical contact occurs.

Most advocates of nonviolent resistance, however, do analyze the nature of the act, not its motive, and most do recommend and use some degree of coercion. Indeed, many nonviolent campaigns represent a carefully calculated escalation of coercion. What they unanimously reject is the threat or use of physical restraint, injury, or destruction of persons or their property.[3] If physical

---

[2] For example, President Richard Nixon has referred to plans that provide incentives for the building of low-income housing in the suburbs as coercive. He calls them forced housing plans.

[3] Some "nonviolent" militants have trapped administrators in their offices, and Father Phillip Berrigan was alleged to have planned a "nonviolent" kidnapping. Both would seem to be doubtful nonviolent resistance tactics. Also, some discussion about the "nonviolent" destruction of property has occurred. Again, the destruction of others' property would not appear to be nonviolent, even if it is preferable to the destruction of their bodies.

restraint, injury, or destruction (or the threat of these) is accepted as an appropriate definition for the term *violence,* then it follows that *nonviolence* is left to encompass a wide range of coercive behavior; it stops short only at the physical. On the other hand, not all acts that have no physical consequences are properly referred to as nonviolent, for to be nonviolent an act must also occur in a context where violent action would generally be considered either legitimate or normal. Nonviolent action, then, implies restraint; it suggests that one deliberately refrains from expected violence. To summarize, nonviolent behavior involves self-control or restraint; it can entail coercion, but not physical violence or the threat of physical violence, and it can also use noncoercive techniques such as persuasion or conversion.

When one persuades or converts another, one changes his opinions or beliefs rather than his options. Any resultant change in behavior, then, is due to a change in inner conviction rather than to a change in external circumstances. A change that is sudden and produced principally by an appeal to the emotions is frequently referred to as a conversion. A change that is the result of reasoned argument and that may take a longer period of time is said to be achieved through persuasion. Attempts to convert and to persuade may be made simultaneously. Both may also be used in conjunction with coercive nonviolent behavior.

Persuasion and conversion are superior agents of change because their effect is usually long lasting. They are not always preferable to coercion, however, for to insist that one's opponent change both his behavior and his convictions is to be extraordinarily demanding. To say that one must believe as well as behave correctly, that one's every action must be undergirded with right belief, is to be dangerously Inquisitional. It can lead to insidious investigations and oath-takings, to intimidation, and to the imposition of one group's beliefs upon another. Indeed, to insist on conversion can be to show utter disrespect for the personality of one's opponent. Further, it is unrealistic to build a strategy based on full agreement, for human action is rooted in habit, indifference, instinct, accommodation, and tolerance, as much as in principle or scruple. Finally, conforming beliefs and attitudes that perfectly integrate the individual and his society not only are hard to effect but also tend to produce social stagnation and inflexibility. In sum, they are often more destructive than beneficial in their total social effect.

In the recent past, the term *nonviolence* was used interchangeably with such terms as *pacifism* and *passive resistance.* Today it has become evident that many persons who refrain from using force in conflict situations are anything but pacific or passive. In recognition of this, a general shift has occurred toward the use of the phrase *nonviolent resistance* to indicate a deliberate policy of refraining from the use of force even while seeking (sometimes very vigorously) to create social change. For this reason *resistance* requires definition. Also, it must be distinguished from *nonresistance, passive resistance,* and *aggression.*

*Nonresistance* describes compliance that is unwilling. This kind of conformity may reflect cowardice or it may reflect a simple utilitarian judgment that the issue involved is not worth the risk or price of resistance.

*Passive resistance* refers to a simple refusal to fulfill some social requirement. Such resistance is frequently individual and unpublicized, but it is not necessarily either. The passive resister acts as he judges best or imperative regardless of external pressures. His primary concern is his own behavior. He does not seek to impose his values upon others, except possibly by setting a good example, nor does he seek to change others' behavior except as it may interfere with his chosen behavior.

*Resistance* involves an attempt to change another's behavior and not simply for one's own benefit. A person who resists acts with concern for others; he takes a risk in order to assist others; he assumes the responsibility or duty of correcting a generally harmful practice. Resistance, therefore, is a social act.[4]

*Nonviolent resistance,* then, is restrained action calculated to change another's behavior for a social purpose without use or threat of physical restraint, injury, or destruction of one's opponent or his property. (One may properly destroy his own property, as the Dukhobors do to dramatize their nonattachment to this world.)

Common sense dictates two additions to this definition. First, as noted before, to be nonviolent an act must occur in a context in which a violent act would be considered appropriate or at least understandable. Second, to be called resistance an act must not follow the regular channels provided by society for the conduct of conflict. Routine behavior cannot be regarded as resistance. A strike for higher wages by a labor union today cannot properly be called resistance for it is a normal part of the bargaining process. On the other hand, the identical action could accurately have been described as resistance in the 1920s.

*Resistance* implies reactive or defensive behavior and suggests that one's opponent is aggressive or offensive (in both senses of the word). But precisely how does one distinguish resistance from aggression? The ordinary way is probably to say that it is *I* who resists, and *he* or *you* who aggresses. The distinction between promoting change and trying to preserve the status quo may be relevant, but any attempt to label one party to a conflict the initiator of the conflict is sure to result in an infinitely regressive exchange of the undesired label *aggressor.* Actually, a precise definition of the term *aggression* is not crucial to a discussion of nonviolence if two things are remembered: (1) In spite of popular prejudice, the Kellogg-Briand Treaty, and the U.N. Charter, neither aggression nor resistance possesses any inherent moral quality; aggression may serve good ends and resistance bad. (2) Nonviolent resistance is not necessarily reactive or defensive. The phrase refers only to a way of waging struggle. It indicates absolutely nothing about which party to a struggle is "right," nor does it indicate which party initiated the struggle.

*Direct action* involves the use of one's physical presence as a part of one's resistance. This may mean only that one does acts of mercy or renders

---

[4] This theme is common to the following: Albert Camus, *The Rebel* (New York: Vintage Books, 1962); Christian Bay, "Civil Disobedience: Prerequisite for Democracy in Mass Society," in *Political Theory and Social Change,* ed. David Spitz (New York: Atherton Press, 1967); and Michael Walzer, "The Idea of Resistance," *Dissent,* Autumn 1960, pp. 369–73.

services. Such action may also mean, however, that one engages in illegal action and this may or may not involve civil disobedience.

*Civil disobedience* may be defined as the deliberate and public infringement of a law recognized by the actor as legal, (that is, as constituted and enforced in accordance with accepted governmental procedures) for the purpose of producing social change.

If a legal violation is unintentional, it does not involve disobedience. If it is clandestine, it is criminal. If the legitimacy of the government that passed the law or is enforcing it is denied, the act is revolutionary. A person who practices civil disobedience does not contest the origin or the authority of a law; he protests its content or its consequences.

The word *civil,* then, appears to have at least two distinct meanings in reference to civil disobedience. First, it means that the government is being disobeyed, and second and more important, it refers to the fact that the person who disobeys regards himself as a citizen—and a loyal and law-abiding one. The disobedient person's view is that loyalty to his state compels him to disobey a particular law in order to better the state. Still, he demonstrates his basic allegiance to his government and can even be said to remain within the boundaries of law, because he publicly acknowledges his misdeed and accepts its legal consequences.

The use of civil disobedience can be quite in accord with noncoercive, nonviolent resistance if the resister accepts his penalty and has as his aim the dramatization of certain conditions through voluntary suffering. (He accomplishes the latter by accepting without complaint the punishment exacted for his disobedience.)

In some cases, however, the resister does not joyfully accept his penalty. Disobedience is not followed by a courtroom plea of "guilty" or "no contest." Instead, the defendant avails himself of any available legal device that will help him escape conviction—no matter how irrelevant the device may be to the main issue. An individual may justify such action on one of the following grounds: the point has been sufficiently dramatized by his arrest; he can be more effective outside of a cell than in; or as long as the system exists one might as well use it. While such behavior does not contradict the basic principles of civil disobedience, wily legal maneuver does dilute any purity of motive attributed to the resister or claimed by him; it also diminishes substantially his claim to have offered self-sacrifice.

Still when resisters practice civil disobedience and then fight their conviction with every legal resource available, motives beyond a failure of nerve may well be present. The aim may be to clog the courts with many cases to obstruct the judicial system. This tactic would also include insisting on lengthy and costly individual jury trials, and complicating and delaying each trial to raise total costs as much as possible. Such behavior is nonviolent, but it involves the changing of options rather than perceptions. Therefore, it is appropriate only to a coercive kind of nonviolent resistance. Another aim might be to make such a mockery of the proceedings so as to totally discredit them. The goal would be to disconnect the public's conceptions of law and of justice—to suggest that law's chief component is force, or legalized violence, rather than equity. Interestingly enough, although the purpose of such a tactic is persuasion rather than coercion, it provokes great hostility. The courtroom performance of the Chicago Seven produced strong emotions; as many of them were critical as laudatory.[5]

Optimally, civil disobedience is directed against an "unjust" law. In practice it may involve the violation of any of many laws in the pursuit of what is thought just. It is only in the most fortunate of circumstances that a resister can directly associate injustice and the enforcement of a particular statute. This is because injustice is as often the result of acts (or statutes) omitted as it is of those committed. It is also because injustice is as frequently the result of private acts and decisions as it is of governmental acts and decisions. This means that individuals pursuing justice often find themselves facing such ignoble charges as vagrancy, failing to obey an officer, or traffic or building code violations. The effect is to dull the edge of what may have begun as a high-minded campaign. The public's attention is diverted from the issue the campaigners are trying to raise; it wonders at their simple lawlessness. At the same time, the normally law-abiding campaigner falters; he is reluctant to make a personal sacrifice for such apparently inconsequential issues, especially when he himself regards the violated law(s) as necessary to civil society.

As long as officials are able to persuade the public and a substantial proportion of the resisters that ordinary laws are being ordinarily administered, civil disobedience will flounder. It is only when the enforcement of law is perceived as a form of attack or perhaps counterattack that the resister's capacity to act, in particular to act illegally, is stimulated. It is only when protesters can demonstrate that the law is the tool of some group rather than an institutionalized decision of the community as a whole that disobedience begins to generalize and to produce that general disrespect for law so feared by opponents of civil disobedience.

Civil disobedience is an obvious way of courting self-suffering or of coercing a society's legal system. Contrary to much public opinion, however, there is no necessary connection between it and nonviolent resistance. A nonviolent resister may never commit civil disobedience and a believer in violence may consciously use it as a prelude to more rugged struggle. Henry David Thoreau, whose eloquent essay (written after he had spent but one night in jail) has probably produced more commitment to civil disobedience than any other piece of literature, was not committed to nonviolence; indeed, he cannot even be said to have practiced civil disobedience as it has been defined here. As to the first point, Thoreau's later though less well-known essay "A Plea for Captain John Brown" is an unequivocal tribute to rebellion and to violence. In it Thoreau notes that Brown held to the "peculiar doctrine that a man has a perfect right to interfere by force with the slaveholder, in order to rescue the slave." He also notes that "I agree with him . . . I do not wish to kill nor to be killed, but I can

---

[5] For Jerry Rubin's account of this trial see *We Are Everywhere* (New York: Harper & Row, Publishers, 1971).

foresee circumstances in which both these things would be by me unavoidable."[6] As to the second point, by his refusal to pay taxes Thoreau was attempting to renounce civil society, not to act with civic responsibility. He wished to avoid, not to fulfill, the consequences of his citizenship; he sought to dissociate himself from his government, not to change its policy.

## Types of Nonviolent Resistance

Many Americans are taught that the use of stereotypes is both ignorant and wrong. Why then is the creation of archetypes considered one of sociology's highest pursuits?

First, typing or classification involves the organization of data into coherent groups. It is the most fundamental of all intellectual tasks, but the part of this activity that requires intelligence is not the sorting but rather the choice of criteria to be used in sorting. The creative activity, then, is the selection of the characteristics by which categories are to be defined.

In general, the basis for selection of criteria is that they are:

1. Clear, precise, and capable of objective application.
2. Correlated with other characteristics so that generalizations can be made about the various categories even though only one or two traits are actually assessed.
3. Meaningful or relevant to one's inquiry.

The derogation of stereotyping comes from the incorrect use of typing information. To be specific, stereotyping usually involves the attributing of a group's characteristics to single individuals who belong to the group. For instance, in the United States today, when ones sees a black male entering the rear door of a $100,000 house one often assumes he is a delivery man, part of a cleaning crew, or a burglar. He could, of course, be the owner, the wife's lover, or an FBI agent. While knowledge of American society suggests the first three possibilities are the more probable, it would be unjust and sometimes incorrect to treat any particular individual as though he were a servant or a criminal without obtaining further information. What is invidious is the application of typical information to individuals, not the creation of typologies.

Many different typologies of nonviolent resistance have been essayed. One approach is to establish categories based on the resister's motive. If one thoroughly analyzes the many motives that may be impelling at the different levels of an individual's consciousness, and if one acknowledges the difficulty of linking particular motives with particular actions, the returns from an inquiry based on this classification might appear to be marginal. Still, it seems worth noting that nonviolent behavior is usually propelled by one of two basic urges. One is the urge to act morally; the other is the desire to accomplish a particular purpose. Sometimes a resister wishes to behave well; sometimes he seeks to act effectively.

---

[6] James Mackaye, *Thoreau: Philosopher of Freedom* (New York: Vanguard Press, 1930), p. 85.

A second way of distinguishing varieties of nonviolent resistance is to consider the resister's intentions towards his opponent. What effect does the resister seek? Has he plans to evade, defy, convert, persuade, or coerce?

In its most passive form, the goal of nonviolent action may simply be to escape the attention(s) of some authority. The resister may only seek to avoid complying with specific demands made of him. An example of this kind of resistance would be refusal to cooperate with the draft.

A purpose more difficult to achieve is that of interaction with one's foe, and thereby changing his behavior through conversion, persuasion, or coercion. In the first two cases, one would try to change the mind of the antagonist. Occasionally an opponent is brought to a wholehearted acceptance of the resister's position, and hence to a change in his own behavior. More often he only develops respect for the resister. That is, he holds to his original position but at the same time he comes to a new perception of the resister as being human, and therefore as holding a legitimate (even if mistaken or limited) point of view. Any resulting change in behavior, then, is based not on a change in belief, but on a willingness to express one's appreciation for a worthy opponent. In the second case, changed behavior is derived from new respect, not from a totally new revelation. The adoption of the nineteenth amendment, regarding women's suffrage, to the U.S. Constitution may have been the result of such a process.

Coercive change is accomplished through penalty, or threat of penalty, or possibly through reward or promise of reward. The way in which a new accommodation is reached is through a bargaining process, in which each party seeks to extract as much as possible from the situation. Because of their mutual dependency, or because of some other social tie, however, neither party wishes to disrupt the relationship entirely. Continued interaction is assumed. This kind of relationship is well illustrated by the tie that exists between employer and employee or between retailer and customer.

Some uneasiness may be felt over the equating of coercion and bargaining; probably this is because bargaining is usually thought of as a mutual process while coercion is thought of as a one-sided kind of activity. Most of the literature on nonviolent resistance does stress unilateral change, and most of it does refer to the two parties in conflict as resister and opponent. However, when a victory is finally proclaimed it is rarely on precisely the terms envisioned or demanded by the "winner." Even though one side or the other may feel that it has won or lost, coerced or been coerced, most cases of conflict resolution actually do involve mutual change. This is because coercion changes behavior by altering social circumstances, and to change these circumstances almost necessarily requires changed behavior on the part of the coercer, although not necessarily in the direction of compromise. For this reason it is not inappropriate, although it may be unusual, to consider coercion as a form of bargaining and bargaining a form of coercion.

A third way of classifying nonviolent resistance is to consider its intended target. Although the public and some practitioners of nonviolent resistance do conceive of it as something that occurs between adversaries, many students of nonviolence not only recognize the existence of third parties but also regard those parties as the actual target of their resistance. Thus, one kind of nonviolence addresses its opponent, while another speaks to third parties. Sometimes the nonparticipants are called upon to render moral judgments, to neutrally determine the "right" and then to prod the consciences of those participants in the struggle who are "wrong." Sometimes they are asked actually to involve themselves, to engage in the struggle, to remove themselves from dispassionate neutrality. Some nonviolent resisters, in short, invite intervention. In doing so, they are not always very fastidious about the kind of intervention that results. Almost all of them welcome the use of coercion on their behalf (for instance, they are willing to profit from legal decisions favoring their cause), and sometimes they even approve the use of violence (private or civil) so long as it is committed by someone else.

The activities of some southern civil rights activists illustrate these points. The strategy frequently used in the South, was first to provoke one's opponent into behavior so barbarous that it could not be overlooked by third parties (in this case northern news media), and then to call on the federal government to intervene with whatever force was necessary to protect rights workers and their clients. The result of this strategy was that individuals who personally abstained from all use of force deliberately provoked violence and then called upon others to physically protect them. In provoking violence, the resister was attempting to make more visible what he regarded as a continuing pattern of behavior. He was not so much trying to change the nature of the relationship between himself and his opponent, as he was trying to make it evident. Further, by renouncing the use of force by and for himself while accepting its benefits when applied by others, he may have been trying to ensure the legitimacy of his cause. He may have wished to be as confident as possible that self-interest had not blinded him. He may well have concluded that if others were willing to use violence on his behalf, then his cause must be just.

Some advocates of nonviolent resistance are less worried about motive, and the precise nature of the effect their acts have, than they are about the kind of action they take. They therefore differentiate the kinds of nonviolent resistance according to the techniques used in its conduct. This is a fourth kind of classification.

Leo Kuper, a student of South African nonviolent resistance, believes that the primary types are noncooperation, which seeks to reduce interaction between interdependents through the use of strikes, boycotts, abstention from balloting and similar devices, and civil disobedience, which seeks to heighten interaction and thus to impel response from an unresponsive authority.[7] Having made this distinction, Kuper then attempts to link these techniques with the particular effects he believes each to have. Noncooperation, he feels, works by building a strong and self-respecting resistance organization that, once established, is able to em-

---

[7] Leo Kuper, *Passive Resistance in South Africa* (New Haven: Yale University Press, 1957), pp. 73–94.

barrass, to inconvenience and finally, to coerce its opponent. Civil disobedience, he believes, works by converting the opponent through an emphatic process. In this case, the foe is made to feel uncomfortable, by having to witness or even to inflict suffering, and therefore he acts to alleviate the primary suffering in order to reduce his own suffering.

Harvey Seifert distinguishes the types of nonviolence in a similar way —that is, according to the technique employed, and he, too, uses the categories of noncooperation and civil disobedience. Seifert, however, makes self-suffering a separate and third category since he appreciates that suffering, law-breaking, and judicial punishment are not necessarily connected.[8]

Another way of describing the techniques of nonviolent action is to refer to them as being constitutional, symbolic, or direct.[9] While this character-ization is not very specific about the form action takes in each category, it does suggest that the important difference between different kinds of nonviolent resist-ance is the degree to which each challenges the legal order. There is also some suggestion that the use of nonviolent action follows (or should follow) an es-calatory pattern of extra and illegal activity. A somewhat similar gradation of nonviolent techniques has been described by Gene Sharp, who describes nonviolent techniques as being rooted in protest, resistance (or noncooperation), or inter-vention.[10]

A fifth way of classifying nonviolent resistance is to consider what groups are involved in the conflict. Such variables as whether the conflict is between one individual and another individual, between an individual and the state, or between one state and another state, are obvious examples. Other cate-gories include the community or society versus the state, the individual versus a private group, and one private group versus another private group.

Still another way of differentiating the varieties of nonviolent resis-tance is according to the degree of calculation involved in their use. In such an analysis the crucial question asked is whether the nonviolence being investigated is spontaneous, tactical, or strategic.[11]

A seventh and final way of classifying the types of nonviolence is to consider the goal pursued. That goal may be nonviolence itself; one's purpose may be to lead a nonviolent way of life. While this way of life has been de-scribed as having a wide variety of utopian qualities, it is nearly always stable in conception and seems usually to be rooted in one of two basic assumptions. Either it is believed that men's relationships are by nature harmonious, or it is argued that all men possess a fundamental unity, which is sometimes said to be based on their oneness, sometimes on their sameness, and sometimes on their commonly shared perceptions.

Alternatively, nonviolent action may be thought of as a way of achiev-ing specific and limited goals. In this case, it is usually not argued that men

---

[8] Harvey Seifert, *Conquest by Suffering* (Philadelphia: Westminster Press, 1965), p. 17.
[9] April Carter, *Direct Action* (London: Peace News, 1962), p. 34.
[10] Sharp's views will be discussed at length in Chapter 4.
[11] This is the view of William Miller, which will be discussed further in Chapter 5.

should and can live together pacifically. On the contrary, it is usually assumed that they cannot, that human conflict is both inevitable and eternal. This being the case, nonviolence is advocated because it is seen as the most economical way to conduct life's continual struggle. From this perspective nonviolent resistance is seen as a civilized test of strength; it is viewed as a sophisticated trial-by-ordeal. Already military strategists of the major powers have learned to ritualize their tests of strength; this they do through guerrilla warfare or through manipulated coups d'état that are carried on or out in smaller or weaker countries. In the same way nonviolent resistance can be described as a further ritualization of human conflict. Indeed, at least one author has specifically discussed the similarities (and dissimilarities) between guerrilla warfare, "symbolic violence," and nonviolent resistance.[12] Those who advocate nonviolent resistance as the utilitarian way to conduct struggle do not, however, adopt a peace-at-any-price position. They are urging warfare, but an economical and humane form of warfare that pursues freedom, justice, human dignity, or other well- or ill-defined but compelling goals without negating the goal pursued.

To separate those views that hold nonviolence itself to be the end from those that hold nonviolence to be a means to an end does not suffice. This is because the view that nonviolence is a means subsumes two quite different perspectives—one of nonviolence as *the* means, and the only means, appropriate to the resolution of conflict, and one of nonviolence as *a* means, one of many appropriate means.

In the first view, nonviolent resistance is advocated as producing the best possible result in all conflict situations. This is often done without specifying exactly what the result will or should be. Its effect is to adopt a "means-justifying-the-end" position. The goal is left unclear, but if it is obtained through the consistent practice of nonviolent resistance, it is thought to be "good" or "true," or the "best or truest possible." In its practical effect, such a view closely approximates the position of those who advocate nonviolence as an end or as a "way of life," for both urge the regular and consistent practice of nonviolence. To view nonviolent resistance as *a* means, however, is to reveal nothing about how often or when one will practice it. That is determined by the goal, for in this case the resister establishes his purpose and then chooses the best method of achieving it. This seems reasonable. To evaluate something properly as a means, one ought to have a clear notion of the end desired. When nonviolent resistance is assumed to be *the* way to meet conflict, virtually any result of nonviolent activity can be said to be the most correct or best conclusion possible. Genuine evaluation of efficacy does not occur because no opportunity is given to offer counterevidence. Only when proponents of nonviolence define their goals before they take action can their success be assessed. Only then can the mixed-mode justification, "It's right and besides that, it works" be fairly tested; for regardless

---

[12] Joan Bondurant, "Paraguerrilla Strategy," *Journal of Conflict Resolution* 7, no. 3 (September 1963): 235–45; and "Satyagraha versus Duragraha: The Limits of Symbolic Violence," in *Gandhi: His Relevance for Our Times,* ed. G. Ramachandran and T. K. Mahadevan (Bombay: Bharatiya Vidya Bhavan, 1964).

of the depth and consistency of one's feeling of commitment, to urge nonviolence as a means is to urge it conditionally. To urge something conditionally, one must be able to make an objective judgment; one must be able to delimit a boundary between results that will be regarded as satisfactory and those that will not be considered satisfactory.

Those who advocate a nonviolent way of life as an end and those who advocate nonviolence as *the* means to the resolution of conflict (because its results are believed always to be superior to what could have been or can be won through the use of violence) combine to form a consistently committed group, sometimes called "principled" proponents of nonviolent resistance.

These principled advocates of nonviolent resistance are often contrasted with "pragmatic" advocates of nonviolence. While the former focus on the nonviolent activity itself, the latter concentrate on the goals they wish to achieve; they evaluate as rationally as possible their chances of succeeding through the use of various types of nonviolent resistance. They ignore, endure, or try to evade any grievances they judge to be not worth the cost of resistance, either because these grievances are insignificant or because they are not susceptible to nonviolent methods.

Some would argue that this position too is principled, for even though it regards nonviolent resistance as only one weapon in a whole arsenal of techniques available for waging conflict, it does entirely rule out the use of violence. This is in contrast to those who view nonviolent resistance as a possible technique, but who are quite willing to use violence if nonviolence fails. While these individuals desire to win as cheaply as possible, they do not set a limit on the means they will use; he who is committed to nonviolent resistance does set a limit. Further, the nonviolent resister often argues that because the possibility of using violence is always in the mind of the uncommitted, they are inhibited both in their capacity to explore fully the possibilities of nonviolence and also in their willingness to take the kind of risks necessary for serious struggle. Their imagination, persistence, and ability to accept suffering, then, are thought to be so impaired as to prevent them from using nonviolent resistance in any but its most obvious and safest form. Pragmatic advocates of nonviolent resistance, do, therefore, renounce the use of force. Unlike principled advocates, however, they think of such resistance as but one of a variety of ways to achieve specific and clearly defined goals. Also, they are acutely sensitive to the prospects of success or failure in particular situations, and they are keenly aware of the costs of conflict.

While each of the distinctions discussed here has been thought basic by at least one student of nonviolent resistance, only one person has made a real attempt to integrate them into a single grand scheme. Gene Sharp is that individual. He has selected six principal characteristics of nonviolence, and more than forty subcharacteristics. He has then attempted to correlate these variables with what he considers to be nine separate types of generic nonviolence. His is a masterful piece of analysis as you may see by the accompanying chart. This design is, however, too unwieldy for convenient use and the discussion to follow will not use it. The categories that will be used are quite simple. They are

## Some Main Characteristics of the Types of Generic Non-Violence

| | Non-Resistance | Active Reconciliation | Moral Resistance | Selective NV | Passive Resistance | Peaceful Resistance | NV Direct Action | Satyagraha | NV Revolution |
|---|---|---|---|---|---|---|---|---|---|
| **1. Attitudes to self and society:** | | | | | | | | | |
| a) "Otherworldly" | Yes | No | No | Maybe | No | No | No | No | No |
| b) "This-worldly" | No | Yes | Yes | Maybe | Yes | Yes | Yes | Yes | Yes |
| c) Concern with own "purity" | Yes | Yes | Yes | Maybe | No | Maybe | Maybe | Yes | Maybe |
| d) Support status quo in society | No | No | No | No | Maybe | Maybe | Maybe | No | No |
| e) Desire to effect a particular social change only | No | No | No | No | Maybe | Maybe | Maybe | No | No |
| f) Desire to effect social reforms, not basic changes | No | Maybe | Yes | No | Maybe | Maybe | Maybe | No | No |
| g) Desire to effect social revolution, i.e., basic changes | No | Maybe | No | Maybe | Maybe | Maybe | Maybe | Yes | Yes |
| **2. Attitudes to "evil":** | | | | | | | | | |
| a) Withdrawal from | Yes | Yes | Yes | Maybe | Maybe | Maybe | Maybe | Yes | Maybe |
| b) Imperative to act against | No | Yes | Yes | Yes | Yes | Yes | Yes | Yes | Yes |
| **3. Attitudes to violence (V) and non-violence (NV):** | | | | | | | | | |
| a) NV based on principle | Yes | Yes | Yes | No | No | No | Maybe | Yes | Usually |
| b) NV based on expediency | No | No | No | No | Yes | No | Maybe | No | No |
| c) NV based on mixed a and b | No | No | No | Yes | No | Yes | Maybe | No | Maybe |
| d) NV regarded as intrinsically good | Yes | Yes | Yes | Maybe | No | Yes | Maybe | Yes | Yes |
| e) NV regarded as a method | No | Yes | Yes | No | Yes | Yes | Yes | Yes | Yes |
| f) NV as a method regarded as a full substitute for V | ...... | Yes | Yes | ...... | Maybe | Yes | Yes | Yes | Yes |
| g) NV regarded as a method which may be used in association with V | ...... | No | No | ...... | Maybe | No | No | No | No |
| h) Personal V in general rejected | Yes | Yes | Yes | No | No | No | No | Yes | Usually |
| i) Group V in general rejected | Yes | Yes | Yes | No | No | No | No | Yes | Yes |
| j) State V in general rejected | Yes | Maybe | Maybe | No | No | No | No | Yes | Usually |
| k) War in general rejected | Yes | Yes | Yes | No | No | No | No | Yes | Yes |
| l) Only certain V rejected as a subsidiary effect of a non-pacifist conception | No | No | No | Yes | No | No | No | No | No |
| m) V regarded as more than physical V, e.g, hostile attitudes | Yes | Yes | Maybe | No | No | Maybe | Maybe | Yes | Yes |

The characteristics attributed to each type are based largely upon the avowals of the respective groups; the section on "Attitudes toward opponents" thus refers to *avowed* attitudes toward opponents, for example. SOURCE: Gene Sharp, "The Meanings of Nonviolence: A typology," *The Journal of Conflict Resolution* 3, No. 1 (March 1959): 65–66. Copyright 1959 by the University of Michigan. Reprinted by permission.

Continued

| | Non-Resistance | Active Reconciliation | Moral Resistance | Selective NV | Passive Resistance | Peaceful Resistance | NV Direct Action | Satyagraba | NV Revolution |
|---|---|---|---|---|---|---|---|---|---|
| **4. Attitude toward opponents:** | | | | | | | | | |
| a) Hatred | No | No | No | Maybe | Maybe | No | Maybe | No | No |
| b) Resentment | No | No | No | Maybe | Maybe | Maybe | Maybe | No | Maybe |
| c) Indifference | No | No | No | Maybe | Maybe | Maybe | Maybe | No | Maybe |
| d) Respect | Maybe | Yes | Yes | Maybe | Maybe | Yes | Maybe | Yes | Yes |
| e) Good will | Yes | Yes | Yes | Maybe | No | Yes | Maybe | Yes | Yes |
| f) Love | Yes | Yes | Yes | No | No | Maybe | Maybe | Yes | Maybe |
| **5. Implementation of the approach:** | | | | | | | | | |
| a) Acts of "self-purification" | Yes | Yes | Maybe | Maybe | No | Maybe | Maybe | Yes | Maybe |
| b) Personal way of living | Yes | Yes | Yes | Maybe | No | No | No | Yes | Maybe |
| c) Persistent friendliness | Yes | Yes | Yes | Maybe | No | Maybe | Maybe | Yes | Maybe |
| d) Acts of mercy | Yes | Yes | Yes | No | No | Maybe | No | Yes | Yes |
| e) Exhortations | Yes | Yes | Yes | Yes | Maybe | Maybe | Maybe | Maybe | Maybe |
| f) "Education" | No | Maybe | Yes | Maybe | No | Maybe | No | Yes | Yes |
| g) Verbal persuasion | Yes | Yes | Yes | Yes | Maybe | Yes | Maybe | Yes | Yes |
| h) Use of state to effect social change | No | Maybe | Maybe | Maybe | No | No | No | No | Maybe |
| i) Use of non-state means to effect social change | No | Yes | Yes | Maybe | Yes | Yes | Yes | Yes | Yes |
| j) "Constructive program" | No | No | No | No | No | No | No | Yes | Maybe |
| k) Passive forms of NV resistance | Rarely | Yes | Yes | Maybe | Yes | No | No | Yes | Yes |
| l) Active forms of NVR and direct action (DA) | No | Maybe | Maybe | Maybe | No | Maybe | Yes | Yes | Yes |
| m) Strategy in the NVR-DA | No | No | Rarely | No | Rarely | Maybe | Yes | Yes | Yes |
| **6. Mechanisms of social change:** | | | | | | | | | |
| a) Persuasion-conversion, leading to policy change | ........ | Yes | Yes | Maybe | No | Yes | Yes | Yes | Yes |
| b) NVR-DA, etc., to create new social situation requiring opponent to reconsider attitudes, etc., leading to policy change | ........ | Maybe | Maybe | No | No | Maybe | Maybe | Yes | Maybe |
| c) Attempting persuasion, etc., but use NVR-DA to force policy change whether or not attitudes first changed | ........ | No | Maybe | Maybe | Maybe | Maybe | Maybe | No | Maybe |
| d) No persuasion, etc.; NVR-DA to force policy change | ........ | No | No | Maybe | Maybe | No | Maybe | No | No |

(1) individual nonviolent resistance, (2) group nonviolent resistance, and (3) combined versions of nonviolent resistance. These groups coincide well with many of the distinctions discussed above and are revealing categories. Further, they are relevant to action and useful for prediction.

# 3   Individual Nonviolent Resistance

*The man who does not know when to die does not know how to live.*

John Ruskin, *Unto This Last*

An explanation makes observations comprehensible and predictions possible. The scientist can observe that when water is heated to 212 degrees Fahrenheit at sea level it boils, and that with an increase in elevation there is a slight decrease in the temperature at which boiling occurs. This kind of information can be useful even if it is never explained. If it is explained, however, one is more likely to remember the original data, to make accurate predictions, to be able to relate one set of phenomena to another, and to be able to formulate hypotheses for investigation. In the case cited above, the generally accepted explanation goes as follows: (1) water molecules are composed of atoms in motion; (2) heat increases motion and therefore increases the number of molecules that break the surface and escape into the air; and (3) at higher elevations there is less atmospheric pressure opposing escape of the molecules, and therefore less heat, with correspondingly reduced motion, is required for boiling. A general theory of this sort enormously expands one's capacity for fruitful action and speculation. One can make good guesses about the effect of container shape and composition; one can even estimate the changes that would occur with the varying of atmospheric conditions, as with use of an oxygen tent or a high pressure chamber.

Acceptance of any explanation rests on two criteria: logical consistency and adequacy to experience. Logical consistency requires that all assumptions be explicitly stated and that conclusions be systematically derivable from them. Adequacy requires that both assumptions and observations be explainable within the framework of the explanation.

Explanations that deal with human beings are frequently more difficult to evaluate than those that deal with physical objects. This is because people's interests and their self-esteem interfere with their ability to analyze critically. It is also true that logical consistency is of real importance to only some people some of the time. Both individuals and populations as a whole can, with complete equanimity, hold contradictory views. They can have contradictory goals, such as clean air and two cars in every garage, or they can desire an end without willing the means, as they do when they demand "the best" in public education without providing the necessary tax revenues. In addition, most people's experience is limited and the generalizations they draw from it inaccurate. This is partly because people expose themselves to only a few sources of information, and partly because they tend to heed only that information that confirms beliefs they already hold. It is human to misperceive or to repress information that contradicts one's conviction. Human attitudes and behavior are consequently very hard to change; rarely is it enough for illogic or error to be demonstrated.

Nevertheless, the more intelligent, or logical and adequate, one's behavior, the more likely one is to be effective. Action based on experience and a clear understanding of relationships stands a good chance of achieving its purposes. For this reason, in order to increase their capacity for intelligent behavior, men do, and should, construct, challenge, and use social explanations.

Social theories are rarely developed in a methodical way but this does not bar their systematic examination. Thus, even though explanations of nonviolent resistance usually come after or are the product of action, the discussion that follows will proceed in an orderly way by first setting forth a group of assumptions, and then deducing from them appropriate action techniques. Next, examples of applied nonviolent resistance will be presented; and finally, an estimate of the chances for success of nonviolent resistance will be offered. The basis of the discussion is wide reading and a certain amount of extrapolation as to what authors "must have meant." It is a simple analysis intended for students, not research scholars, and its wide range means that the territory of a number of disciplines has been invaded but not properly cultivated. Perhaps so much induction has occurred that the author must accept full responsibility and refer to this as "Stiehm's theory of nonviolent resistance." My own feeling, however, is that I have only brought together and made explicit ideas stated or implied many times by many people.

## Assumptions of Individual Nonviolent Resistance

Historically, individual nonviolent resistance has been closely associated with religious conviction. Even today the religious influence is strong, but the interesting thing is that religious beliefs seem to function chiefly as a source of motivation. They are rarely used actually to explain the results of nonviolent resistance. Nonviolent resisters often say that they practice nonviolence because the Bible tells them to do so; also, they may appeal to God for the strength to endure the tribulations associated with nonviolence. If their resistance is successful, they may even in joy and relief thank God, but in spite of all this they do not explain their success in terms of divine intervention. They do not refer to God as a cause. In short, religious rhetoric seems to be used to stimulate people to act nonviolently or as an explanation for their already having acted that way. It is not used to explain the consequences of nonviolent resistance, for in our century, causes are almost always described in secular rather than sacred terms.

Because our primary concern is explanations of nonviolence, because our interest is in its causes and consequences, the discussion in this chapter will be strictly secular—even those theories that come adorned in religious raiment will be treated as though they were secular.

Since assumptions are an explanation's fundamental units, our first charge is to put on display those made in explanations of individual nonviolent resistance. Assumptions are prior to reason and are not susceptible to formal proof. Often they are so buried in the individual's mind that raising them to consciousness is a great intellectual chore. Yet, arduous as the task may be, it is crucial that all an explanation's assumptions be explicitly stated. Only then can an explanation be evaluated for internal consistency; only then can its adequacy to experience be assessed; only then can competing explanations be compared; and this is important, for whether explanations are actually in harmony or in conflict has important consequences for the maintenance of cooperative action.

The primary assumption made in individual nonviolent resistance theory is that separate individuals can and should be studied separately, that one individual's motives and activities and their consequences can appropriately be examined apart from those of other individuals. Since secular explanations of individual behavior are commonly referred to as psychological explanations, this theory of nonviolent resistance could appropriately be called a psychological theory instead of a theory of the individual.

Psychological studies attempt to study individual human beings scientifically. This kind of scrutiny reduces human individuality because what is examined are the ways in which all men are alike. For this reason, social and political theories that focus on the individual are often egalitarian in nature. Statements are made either about *a* human being or about *all* human beings. Man is considered either singly or in general. He is examined as a social atom and he is compared with and related to all other human atoms. Difference and hierarchy are both deemphasized.

The second basic assumption made in individual nonviolent resistance theory is that each individual, although individual, is also related to every other individual through a basic "human unity." This is a crucial assumption, for this unity furnishes the motive for individual nonviolence and also makes successful nonviolent resistance possible. It is what makes men wish to act nonviolently and it is what make nonviolent resistance feasible.

Sometimes it is hard to ascertain precisely what is meant by the phrase *human unity.* Probably this is because it is an a priori, deeply rooted conviction that is not subject to evidential proof. Sometimes the phrase seems literally to mean that man as a species comprises a single living being. Richard Gregg expresses this view when he says that "the human species as a whole may for some purposes be considered a loosely integrated organism."[1] This formulation is useful for two important purposes. First, it explains why one would not wish to do violence. This is because to do violence to another would literally be to do

---

[1] Gregg is the dean of modern U.S. theorists of nonviolence. A specialist in industrial relations, he spent four years in India studying nonviolence during the 1920s. He began writing about nonviolence in the 1930s and has continued to make important contributions right up to the present.

violence to oneself; to kill another would be to commit suicide as much as it would be to commit murder. Second, it provides an explanation for the suffering of the apparently innocent. The explanation goes as follows: If a living organism is injured or afflicted with an infection or disease, the effects are felt throughout the body. Pain and various forms of disequilibrium are not confined to a single site; they are widely distributed and manifest themselves in a number of ways. Similarly, each portion (each individual) of the human organism (species) does not reap what it individually sows. Rather, it shares in the common moral experience of the whole. Thus, while moral mistakes and wrongs are atoned for, payment need not be made by the person who committed a particular misdeed.[2]

A second way that nonviolent resistance theorists express the meaning of human unity is to refer to men as being members of a single world family or world community. This conception is useful because it can account for a great deal of human difference; it can include persons of different sex and age and also people with quite different capacities and points of view. At the same time, this conception emphasizes the strength of those ties that bind men together and the power of those taboos that prohibit the use of violence.

Human unity can also be described as resulting from man's common capacities. As Gregg puts it, men are unified, or bound together, by their universal ability to "think, feel, will, understand and act, and to apprehend spiritual truths."[3] What Gregg does not elaborate on but what is crucial in this statement is the implied assumption that men will think and feel alike, that they will understand, and act similarly, and most important, that they will apprehend the same "truths." According to this formulation, unity can be achieved; it can be achieved because men are generically similar. Unity is not automatically realized, however, because even though the apprehension of "truth" is possible for all, its attainment comes only through intense effort and continuous self-discipline.

A fourth and final way of describing unity is to explain it as a mystical, or transcending, experience; to say that it involves the overcoming of self, of space, and of time; indeed, to say that it encompasses the assimilation of all pairs of opposites. Gregg, for one, argues that there exists a universal human spirit that both transcends individual bodies and also remains immanent in them.[4] To fully understand this argument one may have to have a personal mystical experience. Special as such a communion may be, however, it does not require conventional religious practice or belief.

To summarize, advocates of individual nonviolent resistance assume that each individual is worthy of separate consideration and that there exists an underlying or potential human unity. They go on to argue that realization of this unity is desirable and that nonviolent resistance is an appropriate means to it.

The belief that the achievement of human unity is desirable must be

---

[2] Richard Gregg, *The Power of Nonviolence* (Nyack, N.Y.: Fellowship Publications, 1962), pp. 10, 71, 129–30.
[3] Ibid., p. 10.
[4] Richard Gregg, *The Self Beyond Yourself* (Philadelphia: J. B. Lippincott Co., 1956), p. 152.

taken as given. The belief that nonviolent resistance is a means to that unity is argued as follows. First, because unity is real, although unperceived, conflict is illusory. What is required to "end" it, then, is no more and no less than a changed perception—a new view, a reconceptualization. Such a conflictless vision is always attainable because unity exists, but rethinking is always necessary because an ever-changing physical and social environment produces ever-changing images of reality. Thus advocates of individual nonviolent resistance expect conflict to appear and to reappear; this they find inevitable but not disheartening for they believe reality can always be communicated.

If widely experienced feelings of conflict are less real or at least less significant than rarely experienced feelings of oneness, the revelation of unity's existence should be all that is needed to shrivel any and all conflicts into nothingness. It would seem, then, that the disclosure of mankind's oneness is the essence of individual nonviolent resistance.

If a political actor wishes to channel his energies into a demonstration of man's unity, he will have to give much consideration to the wishes and perceptions of the parties involved in conflict. Then he will have to restructure the situation so that issues are seen in a new way, one that is broader, more fundamental, or more long-range. His goal in creating these perceptions will be to induce opponents to see themselves as kin.

### Aims of Nonviolent Action

How do theorists of individual nonviolent resistance think that such perceptions can best be created? By acting out the assumptions of nonviolent resistance, by constantly and absolutely according respect to each individual personality—one's own and that of all others. If conflict can be expected to dematerialize in the face of complete respect for self and others, if unity, or harmony, coincides with full individuality, if the whole can be seen only if every part recognizes and is recognized, then appropriate nonviolent acts fall into one of four categories. The categories are based on acts that (1) pay respect to others, (2) strengthen self-respect of others, (3) build one's own self-respect, and (4) earn the respect of others for oneself. To be briefer, the essence of nonviolent action seems to be to pay respect, promote everyone's self-respect, and win respect.

It must be remembered that to those committed to individual nonviolent resistance, respect is absolute and universal. Because it is absolute, one is required to honor the acts, the speech, and even the fancies of each individual. One must be careful not even to force consideration of a new idea on others because even the mildest compulsion can be considered a form of violence. Yes, even those persons who wish to engage in violence are to be respected and permitted to have that experience so that they can be true to themselves. Even those people who will war should not be stayed, according to proponents of this kind of nonviolence.

Even though the theory of individual nonviolence cites total unity as its goal, it is, in a way, an extremely narrow perspective: it focuses on relationships that exist among individuals—usually on the relationship between two individuals. Thus, exquisite concern is expressed for the self-respect even of those who are violent, although little concern may be registered for those third parties on whom violence may be wreaked. Similarly, while extraordinary admonitions are made to the nonviolent resister in cautioning him against forcing so much as an idea on someone else, massive, painful, and destructive uses of force may be permitted to others. In short, the absolute nature of the individual nonviolent resister's commitment may lead him to an apparently petty and overly meticulous focus on himself, his intentions, and his behavior. To others, he may appear to be quite unmindful of the consequences of his action, or more often, of his inaction. Still, this kind of resister does not see himself as narcissistic. His view is that exemplary behavior is, in the long run, the surest way to reduce violence. He contends that anything less than pure and absolute nonviolence will have a serious and violent backlash effect. He believes literally that like begets like.

Respect must be universal as well as absolute. No human can be defined as inhuman, and therefore excludable. Respect must be paid to those judged insane or criminal; esteem must also be granted to individuals from all classes, castes, and cultures. Every human being must be assumed to be receptive to nonviolent techniques no matter what the circumstances. This means that nonviolent resistance should be used whether the conflict is domestic or international. It means that it is as appropriately used against foreigners burning the White House (which has happened) as it is against amusement park operators refusing to allow integrated patronage of their ferris wheels. Both Hitler and Gandhi and the followers of each should merit nonviolent treatment.

While carefully respecting others and patiently nourishing their self-respect, the nonviolent resister must be careful not to treat himself disparagingly. He must not only maintain his intellectual and moral integrity, but also demonstrate his self-regard even in such small details and mundane ways as the maintenance of cleanliness and proper nutrition. At the same time he must constantly guard against lapsing into one of the perverted forms of self-esteem—self-glorification or self-righteousness.

Paying respect and maintaining self-respect are both fully within the control of the nonviolent resister; the winning of respect is not, and the art of nonviolence is likely to meet its severest tests in this sphere. Here the resister must most carefully calculate his technique, and here the relationship between ends and means, and causes and effects requires the most precise definition.

Theorists of nonviolent resistance discuss both ends and means and causes and effects, and it may be that these phrases are logically interchangeable. The associations they produce, however, are rather different. Indeed, word order alone suggests that he who discusses ends and means is focused on the product of an action, while the use of the phrase "cause and effect" directs attention to an act's origin. Also, the phrase "ends and means" is usually used in the context of a political or philosophical discussion that occurs prior to action, assumes one has control over the means, and admits a degree of doubt as to whether the advocated ends will, indeed, proceed from the advocated means. In contrast, "cause and effect" often occurs in a scientific explanation of something that has already happened, may or may not be controllable, and involves no element of uncertainty. In a discussion of nonviolent resistance, the usual pattern is that in advocating commitment to nonviolence the resister usually refers to ends and means. In explaining the working of nonviolence, however, he should, and often does, discuss causes and their effects.

The very language of explanation, then, is different from that of exhortation. For example, Richard Gregg has been particularly anxious to establish the scientific foundations of nonviolence. As a result, his principal work, *The Power of Nonviolence,* is filled with cause-and-effect terminology. The language of Newtonian physics is especially prominent. Nonviolence is discussed in terms of moral dynamics, psychic energy, the resolution of forces and the use of leverage, position, poise, and power; reference is made to fulcrums, instruments, and balance. This kind of metaphor imparts a sense of reality to things that are immaterial, but more important, it suggests there is a cause-effect relationship involved in events that may not generally be thought to be related—at least not in a clear and unambiguous manner.

The crucial question remains. What can the nonviolent resister do that will cause others to respect him; what can he do that will have the effect of creating respect for him in others?[5]

Paying respect seems to be one way of securing respect. Apparently there is a tendency to like people who like you, to trust people who trust you, and to esteem people who esteem you. This is the basis of the individual nonviolent resister's argument that good feeling can be deliberately produced by displaying good feeling, that there is a mirroring effect that can be consciously used to create specific behavior. Experiments have been conducted to see if empirical data would support this assertion. Pitirim Sorokin, who was the director of the Harvard Research Center in Creative Altruism, believed that amitology, the science of love, was a science that could and should be experimentally validated. In one of his experiments, Sorokin used five pairs of college students to test the mirroring principle. In each pair, one person, the subject, was instructed to do good deeds on behalf of the other person, whom he did not particularly like, for an eight-month period. The goal was to see if acting as though you liked a person would make him like you, and you like him; in short, to see if conscientious liking behavior could produce genuine mutual liking. Sorokin claimed his results showed that it did.[6]

Few advocates of nonviolence consider social imitation a sufficient cause for the winning of respect. For this reason they supplement the paying of respect with other devices. One of them is to demonstrate strength. Strength can be displayed either by showing the intense commitment of a single individual or

---

[5] No progress can be made unless one is respected at least enough so that his existence is acknowledged. The fiercest union battles were for recognition; similarly, feminists today find their first problem is to be taken seriously.

[6] Pitirim Sorokin, ed., *Forms and Techniques of Altruistic and Spiritual Growth* (Boston: Beacon Press, 1954), ch. 26.

of a few individuals, or by showing the close association of a large number of individuals. In a simple matter like picketing, intense commitment can be demonstrated by sustained picketing (hours, days, weeks, months) or by long-distance marching, which is both physically fatiguing and done at the expense of one's ordinary affairs. Similarly, strength in numbers can be shown either through simultaneous mass action, or if resisters wish to demonstrate strength but not to appear threatening, through long-continued sequential action. Recent antiwar demonstrators have used all these techniques. They have maintained lengthy vigils; they have gone long distances, including as far as Hanoi; they have filled the streets of Washington in the amount of hundreds of thousands; and they have participated in single-file candlelight marches, each marcher representing a man killed in Vietnam.

A third method used by nonviolent resisters to invoke respect is to utilize an empathic process for the communication or transfer of their own feelings of self-regard to their opponents. In this process, the respect one accords oneself is used to produce a similar respect in others. This does not involve an exchange of respect; rather it involves duplication. The opponent imitates the resister's own feelings. He respects the resister because the latter respects himself. Since the mirroring and duplication processes both serve to reduce conflict, their different nature—the paying of respect to another and the paying of respect to oneself— is frequently overlooked. As yet no theoretician has adequately explained which circumstances can be expected to produce an exchange of feelings and which should be expected to provoke an imitation of feelings, or whether both effects can occur simultaneously. Still, both seem to be ways of winning respect.

Nonviolent resisters use self-respect to reduce conflict in one final way. They stress the ways in which they are like their foe; they emphasize similarities. If the foe respects himself, the argument goes, he will have to extend his respect to those he perceives as like himself.

While the nonviolent resister is consistently counseled to practice perfect respect for each individual personality, and while such behavior is thought to reduce conflict, the ultimate goal of nonviolence is not simply civil bilateral relationships, but human unity. To achieve this goal, thought on nonviolence must perceive more than numerous single units. Nor can "compromises," "balances," or "resolved forces" produce the concept of a unified whole. To reach this perception, theorists of individual nonviolent resistance turn to other kinds of phrases such as "the achievement of synthesis," or "the realization of integration." Their meaning is that to peacefully end conflict no one and nothing can be cancelled out; what is required, instead, is incorporation. This describes precisely the goal of individual nonviolence: the inclusion of everyone and everything, and the restructuring or redefining of the situation so that difference is muted and conflict surmounted.

## The Power of Individual Nonviolent Resistance

The most distinctive thing about individual nonviolent action is that it is noncoercive. It concentrates on the changing of perceptions rather than on the changing of options. Still, it is not a passive kind of activity. It engages in strenuous mental restructuring and it describes its activity in potent terminology.

It aims at being powerful and so describes itself. Sometimes it is even suggested that real and evident effects have been caused by real, if invisible, forces. Gregg, for example, has described the power of nonviolent resistance as being similar to the unseen powers of electricity, bacteria, enzymes, and symbols. What are the sources of the mysterious power attributed to individual nonviolent resistance? One source is certainly the depth, the sincerity, and the totality of the commitment of the resister. Because his whole being—"body, mind, will and spirit—is integrated and at work with singleness of purpose," he is said to command "immense and unpredictable resources of energy."[7]

A second power source is superior knowledge. If an individual thoroughly understands human psychology, he is more likely to succeed in conveying to other persons his message (in this case, of human unity) than an individual who communicates in only the most conventional way. Even though the successful nonviolent resister will not possess full knowledge of man's nature, he is practically, if not theoretically, well versed in the subtle aspects of communication. It is clear that the practical tips offered in manuals for nonviolent resistance use findings concerning gesture language and other forms of nonverbal communication. The work of psychiatrists such as Jurgen Ruesch and Gregory Bateson and sociologists such as Erving Goffman has much in common with the Friends' series of Pendle Hill pamphlets.

A third way serious resisters enhance their power for nonviolent resistance is by consciously developing a variety of nonviolent habits. The purpose of this training is to ensure a nonviolent response that is conscious yet automatic— one that will occur regardless of external stress or proffered temptation. Training in nonviolent resistance requires training in behavioral as well as intellectual responses because such resistance involves restraint. Nonviolent resistance does not seem to be an instinctual response; therefore, voluntarily accepted or self-imposed discipline becomes essential. Neither education, which provides understanding but does not extend to action, nor organization, which is effective only in a well-structured situation, is sufficient. Individual training in individual responses is necessary because "it is easier to act yourself into a new way of thinking than to think yourself into a new way of acting."[8]

The prescribed discipline can be quite rigorous. Gregg recommends a fourfold discipline encompassing all aspects of human nature. For the body he prescribes work; for the emotions, song and dance; for the mind, study and discussion; and for the spirit, meditation.

Work is basic to nonviolent resistance, and fulfills two crucial functions. One is that it disciplines the individual and accustoms him to nonviolent behavior. The second is that it serves as a form of nonverbal communication, since work done usually takes the form of service. As such it becomes a concrete

---

[7] Gregg, *Nonviolence*, pp. 47, 113–14.
[8] Albert Mehrabian, *Tactics of Social Influence* (Englewood Cliffs, N.J.: Prentice-Hall, 1970), p. 143.

expression of one's feeling of human unity and of one's regard for the personality of others.

Similarly, song, dance, rhythmic exercise, communal dining, and "not too competitive" games are thought to expand one's feeling of human unity beyond those who are nearest and dearest, and to prepare the nonviolent register to incorporate even his most vigorous opponent within his concept of "brother."

Although behavioral training and emotional involvement are given the main emphasis in most training for nonviolent resistance, a full preparation should include intellectual understanding of the philosophy of nonviolence, and its requirements and implications.[9] The reason that intellectual understanding is not more emphasized may be that it has not yet been achieved. Even the classics, the fundamental texts in nonviolence, are primarily descriptive or hortatory. They provide some analysis, and they certainly yield material for analysis, but few approach a systematic explanation of the mechanism—or more likely, mechanisms —through which nonviolent resistance works.

The process of meditation is another important part of the training for individual nonviolence. Its purpose is to achieve a discipline of what Gregg (like many other theorists of nonviolence) refers to as spirit. The secularist would probably describe the purpose as achieving control of the subconscious as well as the conscious aspects of one's mind. In describing what one does in meditation, Gregg explains that one can either focus exclusively on a single idea or attempt to dismiss everything from one's mind—that is, one can try to drive out all thoughts, even all sense impressions. The goal is control, because control increases power.

While thorough training is crucial to the individual nonviolent resister, he does not expect to rely exclusively on his own resources. He augments his power by not perceiving the scope of any particular conflict too narrowly. He does not see it as "him and me": third parties are brought into the picture, for even though the rhetoric of nonviolence may feature only the two parties in opposition to one another, third parties have always been important to any explanation of nonviolent resistance.

Some theorists seek third-party intervention; others, however, wish to use third parties only in a limited way. They use them as significant others, as dispensers of social approval and disapproval. This gives the resister a certain amount of control over even his most powerful opponent for all men are social beings and not social isolates, and even the most powerful rulers continually test and react to the winds of public opinion. Both elites and revolutionaries try to be expert "weathermen."

Especially for the individual nonviolent resister, the attention of outsiders rather than their action is sought. One reason outside observers are valued

9 Among the most available, most authoritative, and most used educational materials in this field are Richard Gregg, *The Power of Nonviolence;* William Miller, *Nonviolence;* Joan Bondurant, *The Conquest of Violence;* Gene Sharp, *Exploring Nonviolent Alternatives;* Thoreau, *Civil Disobedience;* and Martin Luther King, *Stride Toward Freedom.* See the bibliography for other significant works.

is that their view is thought to be unbiased; it is assumed that it accurately reflects the conflict situation. Each party to the conflict can thereby obtain as reliable
a view of the struggle as if he were able to step outside himself and see himself
as others see him. The nonviolent resister who believes he has truth on his side,
then, is not afraid of news coverage. He invites it—especially TV coverage with
its direct access to a mass audience. Indeed, the nonviolent resister may spend
much of his time planning how to attract such scrutiny for he believes his opponents would change their behavior if they knew it would be displayed on network
TV. Men who smash cameras, he would say, wish to hide from themselves.[10]

A second way of describing the role of third parties might be to say
that they serve as nondirective psychotherapists. A nondirective psychotherapist
is one who influences a patient and actually changes his behavior simply by drawing
his attention to his own actions. The assistance provided may consist essentially of
repeating the patient's own statements. "You wonder if others might think you
selfish? You find you cannot sleep well on Saturday nights?" The spectator, in
sum, does not have to take any action; he does not have to make any assessment
or evaluation, yet he can have an important effect simply by serving as a reflecting
surface that demonstrates to each actor the nature of his behavior.[11]

Finally, there are some advocates of individual nonviolence who
seem to believe that the power of nonviolence is continually being augmented
through a process of social evolution. They argue that the fundamental conditions
promoting human survival have now changed and that violence-producing feelings
such as anger and fear are no longer functional. They conclude, therefore, that
such emotions, and even violence itself, are decreasing and will continue to
decrease in incidence. Some even argue that the reason that Eastern civilizations
came to use nonviolence before Western societies is because of their longer social
experience and their denser populations. They believe, in any event, that the
West is now ready for nonviolence because nuclear weapons have made international warfare counterproductive and because our industrialized society has
provided domestic governments with a similarly prohibitive destructive capacity.
Marshall McLuhan has even suggested that twentieth-century improvements in
mass communication and transportation have combined to create a new "global
village," and a village is a community unit that does not usually permit internal
violence.[12]

## Techniques of Individual Nonviolent Resistance

### Introduction

It has been established that individual theories of nonviolent resistance
usually find no justification for coercion. Their recommended actions are restricted

---

[10] Network TV news was clearly of great help to the Southern civil rights movement. It is
not so clear what its effect has been in Northern riot situations. However, in such situations
police have singled out and attacked photographers both in Cleveland and in Chicago.
[11] Gregg, *Power of Nonviolence,* pp. 45–48. See also pp. 77 and 86 and "Satyagraha as a
Mirror" in *Gandhi: His Relevance for Our Times,* ed. G. Ramachandran and T. K.
Mahadevan (Bombay: Bharatiya Vidya Bhavan, 1964).
[12] The work of ethnologist Konrad Lorenz, who has made a similar argument, will be
discussed in Chapter 5.

to the persuasive. This seems reasonable, if for no other reason than because a single individual can hardly expect to employ coercion as his customary modus operandi. Individual resistance has one of two goals: either to communicate the message of human unity to one's opponent, or alternatively to cause him to perceive that unity by himself.

While a desire to communicate seems sufficiently human and humane, it is sometimes not quite so clear that one is fully respecting his opponent's integrity when one "causes" him to perceive. Nonviolent resisters are very purposive in their behavior, and sometimes they do describe their resistance as manipulative. Still, they are generally wary of human engineering and believe that men should be treated as ends, not as things or means. In the resister's view it is not manipulation simply to try to activate that bit of humanity, that "spark of good spirit," that "fineness," that they know to reside in each human heart. They see their only goal as revealing to an individual his innate integrity. Changes in perception, in thinking, or in action that follow, then, are not the product of coercion but the natural consequence of the individual's having recognized his own humanity.

## The Stages of Individual Nonviolent Resistance

While changes in attitude or behavior often seem to be instantaneous and are sometimes described as conversions, they can usually be seen to involve several distinct changes, which appear to occur in stages. In the first stage the resister disarms his opponent. He unsettles him; he throws him off balance; he makes him unsure.[13] One dramatic way of doing this is to refuse to conform to the expectations of one's opponent, to behave well when ill is expected or when ill has been done. Gregg has coined the phrase "moral jiu-jitsu" for such behavior, and it seems an apt phrase, since the resister's lack of opposition is used to upset or unbalance his attacker.

Once the opponent experiences self-doubt, his capacity for action diminishes; he loses his initiative; he becomes hesitant; he may be demoralized. The resister has accomplished his first goal. It is the same as the first goal of conventional warfare: to sap the opponent's will, to soften his resolution. Gregg has described this stage as one in which the resister creates within his foe "a strong new impulse that is incompatible with his previous tendency."[14] This coincides almost exactly with a phenomenon psychologists now refer to as cognitive dissonance. According to this theory, which was developed by Leon Festinger, individuals who experience contradictory or dissonant cognitions are uncomfortable. They experience a "strain toward consistency." They will consciously or unconsciously attempt to reconcile conflicting knowledges by adopting new attitudes that reduce dissonance. These new attitudes may easily yield new behavior. The nonviolent resister, then, deliberately tries to create dissonance in his opponent.

---

[13] This often leads to increased tension and antagonism. These are often prerequisites for change and not necessarily to be avoided. See Gordon Allport, "Catharsis and the Reduction of Prejudice," in *Journal of Social Issues* 1, no. 3 (August 1945): 3–10.

[14] Gregg, *Power of Nonviolence*, p. 53.

He tries to impart new and unsettling perceptions to his foe. Often he does this by returning good for evil, by refusing in any way to represent a threat even if he is himself threatened. This makes it hard for his antagonist to justify the use of force; he cannot claim to be either a potential victim or a benevolent protector of others. He is, in short, disarmed.

The importance of surprise is mentioned again and again in discussions of this first stage of nonviolent action. If this is interpreted to mean novelty, an obvious and severe limitation would be placed on the regularity with which one could resort to this kind of resistance. If, however, one interprets surprise to mean only that nonviolent resistance works by setting up a dissonance between an opponent's expectations and his perceptions, then the description would seem accurate and no frequency limit would be involved.

The second phase of nonviolence concentrates on reassurance of the unnerved enemy. In the beginning of this stage the opponent's balance has been lost; he is emotionally torn; he is unsure of the propriety of any particular response; in short, his nerve has failed. The resister then acts to reduce his insecurity by suggesting to him: that he (the opponent) is a man of integrity whose personality the resister will always respect regardless of the circumstances; and that there are grounds for reaching an accord, that a possibility for resolving the conflict does exist.

In the third and final stage this resolution occurs. Contrary positions are reconciled through interaction of the opponents. It is no longer simply a matter of the resister's manipulation of the foe; instead, both sides are absorbed in an inclusive synthesis. Both derive satisfaction from a situation that has been reordered, so that the former opponents see themselves not as antagonists but as dissimilar parts of a larger whole. This integration indubitably falls short of that ultimate integration desired by Gregg and certain mystic theorists. For them, the final transcendence would be realized only in "the meeting, interaction and blending of the essential qualities of both sides of any pairs of opposites . . . good and evil, past and future, subject and object, creation and destruction, man and woman."[15] Most nonviolent resisters seem to find a simple cessation of conscious struggle sufficient.

## Methods of Nonviolent Resistance

What techniques have resisters found useful in unsettling, reassuring, and reorganizing their foes, in dramatizing to them the fact of man's underlying unity? One way is to startle, to commit the unorthodox in order to create significant emotional impact. A second way is to use gentle but persistent stimulation over a very long period of time, seeking only eventually to change behavior. Often it is argued that a prolonged and subtle pressure is preferable because it is less likely to produce a backlash. Such a reaction is said to occur when an apparently responsive opponent suddenly reverses his field, in reaction usually to a particular

---

[15] Ibid., p. 57; *Spirit Through Body*, pp. 32–36.

and unpleasant incident, and urgently insists upon his original principles. The backlash can, however, be explained in another way. It can be argued that the "backlasher" was never responsive, but that he found it more convenient to object to the style or manner of his opponent than to his argument. It has also been argued that the backlash is just a part of the unsettling process of the first stage, and that it represents insecurity and disturbance and is a sign that change is beginning. Yet another argument against long-term, low key action is that it is very hard to evaluate, especially because its advocates keep saying that success is imminent.[16]

While nonviolent resisters do not suggest the use of hypnosis, they clearly do try to use the power of suggestion. They do so by asserting positively and often that something is true, hoping in this way to persuade their opponent that it is true. For example, a resister may assert "I know that you have the best interests of everyone in mind" so frequently that the opponent finally does begin to let general interests rather than his own particular ones control his action. Thus, the suggestion becomes true as the result of its being believed true, and it is believed true because it was first assertd as true.[17]

This phenomenon has been discussed as an agent of social causation by the sociologist Robert Merton, who has labeled it "the self-fulfilling prophecy." Merton's formulation is somewhat narrow, for he focuses on originally erroneous statements that became true because they were believed. In addition, most of the examples he cites concern unsocial results (the belief that a bank is failing causing a run, which does indeed cause it to fail; or the belief that another country is an enemy, causing one to treat it as such and thus making it one), although there is no inherent reason why a self-fulfilling prophecy should produce such results. The nonviolent resister, for one, proposes to use the self-fulfilling prophecy in order to produce positive results. In addition, he does not affirm untruths; rather, he is most often dealing with ambiguous information or ambivalent feelings.

Nonviolent resisters recognize that, with regard to acceptance, the source of a suggestion is often as important as its content. For this reason, an effort is usually made to use spokesmen who are already respected or admired; or minimally, an effort is made to inspire respect and admiration for him who does the suggesting. It is also recognized that to be fully and continuously effective the suggestion must be internalized; it must derive its energy from the opponent himself. After all, resistance cannot be called successful if the resister must continuously supply the stimulus for his opponent's good behavior.

Individual nonviolent resisters use all conceivable forms of communication to transmit their message of unity. Appeals are made both to reason

---

[16] Recent work on conditioned learning suggests that neither abrupt nor sustained rewards are as effective as intermittent rewards. Apparently men perform best in uncertain situations! See John Mann, *Changing Human Behavior* (New York: Charles Scribner's Sons, 1965), p. 59, and also Mehrabian, *Tactics,* pp. 19–20.

[17] Kuhn provides an interesting discussion of the way people are controlled by what others expect of them. What is crucial is not how one identifies himself but how others identify him. See Manford H. Kuhn, "The Reference Group Reconsidered," in *Symbolic Interaction,* ed. Jerome Manis and Bernard Meltzer (Boston: Allyn and Bacon, 1967), p. 183.

and to emotion. Both abrupt and dramatic and sustained and subtle appeals are made. In addition, the resister consciously attempts to reach his antagonist's subconscious, and he uses nonverbal as well as verbal forms of communication. The aim is to "go deeper than logic," to bring about "illumination." But the unconscious is not exalted, nor reasoning abandoned. The individual resister insists only that reasoning and conscious verbal communication do not suffice; he argues only that all forms of communication must be tried and exhausted.

Voluntary suffering is one way of communicating one's common humanity to foe or to onlooker. It is also a technique which is unique to nonviolent resistance. Its advocates explain that injustice creates suffering, that men hate suffering and will act to alleviate it, and that therefore men will act to correct injustice if the suffering it causes is demonstrated to them.

This argument is complicated by several factors. First, not all suffering is derived from injustice. Its source may be something as mundane as chicken pox or a broken leg. Moreover, some suffering may be considered quite just (even by the afflicted), such as the remorse experienced by a person who has publicly, and as it develops falsely, accused a friend of a felony, or the embarrassment and financial loss suffered by an individual who has been fined for drunken driving. Thus, the nonviolent resister must be able to demonstrate not only that suffering exists but also that it is the product of injustice.

A second difficulty lies in the fact that not all suffering can be alleviated. Some suffering may be due to a lack of abundance, some to inner grievances not susceptible to treatment, and some to that unfortunate, random wrong that is the cost of a necessarily imperfect but organized social system. Men have learned that they must either ignore or accommodate themselves to some human suffering. Therefore, an advocate of voluntary suffering is charged with the duty of showing not only that suffering exists and that it is unmerited, but also that it is unnecessary.

How can the existence of suffering be demonstrated? It has already been suggested that one way to accomplish this is to dramatize suffering, perhaps by converting its form from mental to physical. In the case of the lunch-counter sit-ins, the invisible humiliation of being refused service was sometimes converted to the visible suffering involved in physical attacks against the protesters, and sometimes to the even more intense suffering of incarceration. In either case, the suffering of the excluded became more evident.

A nonviolent resister may be able to show that suffering is unmerited by voluntarily assuming a risk to which he would not ordinarily be subject. Again, in the lunch-counter situation this would be accomplished by having a white person insist upon sharing the fate of a prospective black diner. Some theorists argue that even suffering that is not deliberately sought can be used by the nonviolent resister if his acceptance of it is sufficiently active, and if he acts as though his suffering is voluntary. It seems, however, that to be most effective, "voluntariness" must have some sort of a golden mean. For instance, in our society, to inflict as extreme a suffering on oneself as self-immolation or to go too far in inviting or provoking suffering is to stimulate horror or disgust rather than sympathy.[18] Similarly, to accept or submit to suffering too passively can make one appear servile and contemptible. To be most effective voluntary suffering must be used temperately.

Finally, a nonviolent resister must show that his suffering is unnecessary, that it can be alleviated, and that while the relationship between himself and his opponent will presumably be altered, his opponent will not suffer as a result. In the case of the sit-ins, it is clear that one thing the demonstrators sought to prove was that business would not decrease even if lunch counters were integrated, that exclusion was not economically necessary. Suffering, then, has a dual nature: it is a sign of injustice, and it can also be used as an instrument of change; it is a grievance, but one that can be used to help provide for its own relief.

The two mechanisms through which voluntary suffering and other forms of nonverbal communication work are sympathy and empathy.[19] Both are involuntary responses evoked in those who witness suffering. Sympathy is a feeling *for* someone else and stimulates compassionate or alleviating action. This response is asserted to be universal, although it seems evident that prejudice, custom, or hostility can inhibit it. Still, if sympathy is universal, the nonviolent resister can argue that potentially anyone—even persons like Hitler's Nazis—can be reached and swayed.

Empathy appears to be different from sympathy in that it involves an unconscious imitation *of* another rather than a feeling for another. In the case of voluntary suffering, empathy can be said to work by producing in the onlooker an unconscious imitation of observed suffering. This imitative suffering causes a degree of actual suffering in the observer and he then acts to alleviate his own pain, either by giving succor to the sufferer or by attempting to withdraw from the stimulus.

The nonviolent resister also tries to use empathy in a more positive way, through the practice of moral action. He acts well, hoping that others will follow, at least to some degree, the example he has set. With this technique, a resister can hope to brake or even reverse an escalating spiral of violence. He can hope that his consistent nonviolent action will reproduce itself through the mechanism of empathy and thus cut through a chain of violent actions. Acts of service are especially recommended to those resisters who hope to move others to imitation.

Empathy has still a third use in nonviolent resistance. That is to communicate to an actor what an onlooker's view of his behavior is. As noted previously, it is frequently the perceptions of impartial observers rather than those of the nonviolent resister that are directed at the actors. Empathy's

---

[18] The death of Norman Morrison, a Quaker who burned himself to death to protest the Vietnam War, did not have a strong effect on public opinion. Also, two teenagers, Joan Fox and Craig Badiali, killed themselves as a war protest. Their deaths were almost completely hushed up. Their sacrifice was considered an aberration. See Eliot Asinof, ed., *Craig and Joan: Two Lives for Peace* (New York: Viking Press, 1971).
[19] Max Scheler offers an elaborate treatment of sympathy and empathy in his *The Nature of Sympathy* (London: Routledge and Kegan Paul, 1954).

function here is to encourage better behavior by permitting people to see themselves as others see them. If the perception of the others is disapproving, shame should lead to improved behavior.

The regular use of role-playing in training for nonviolence, or the playing out of all the roles involved in a nonviolent resistance situation, further emphasizes the importance empathy plays in the theory. According to experts, role-playing fulfills a number of functions simultaneously. First, the spontaneous responses it encourages bring things known at the unconscious level to one's conscious level of understanding—both things concerning oneself and things concerning others. Second, role-playing can serve as a tension-releasing device; pent-up aggressions can be acted out. Third, it provides a safe environment for experimenting with new behavior patterns. Fourth, it presents an opportunity to rehearse planned responses.

Both empathy and sympathy involve communication through activity rather than through words. Words can accompany the activity or they may be dispensed with entirely. Probably the most characteristic form of nonviolent action is voluntary suffering that works through both sympathy and empathy. Also important are acts of service, which may be either the product of sympathy or which may be deliberately used by a resister who hopes to elicit imitative behavior through empathy.

The very close connection among language, thought, and action, and their mutual influence, are constantly emphasized in the literature on nonviolent resistance. Action is not thought of as simply the product of thought; it is conceived of also as a mode of thought. Deeds are seen sometimes to precede, sometimes to clarify, sometimes even to produce thought. This means that activities undertaken for one set of reasons often produce further reflection and then yield quite different activities based on a new set of reasons.

Action is also important because it speaks louder than words. It expresses deeper involvement. For both these reasons—because of its effect on thought and because it demonstrates seriousness—nonviolent resisters rightly insist on the importance of committing oneself to action. To act increases one's communication with others, and just as important, it clarifies and confirms one's views to oneself. It is believed that those who lack such clarification and confirmation, those who fail to act routinely on their principles, are persons who will abandon those principles when under stress. It has already been noted that large numbers of pacifists forsake their principles once violence has begun. World War II changed the minds of Bertrand Russell and Albert Einstein, among others. At least some of those who maintained their pacifism felt that wartime falling away was related to the degree to which individual men engaged themselves in regular nonviolent activity. Commitment that is strictly intellectual and not reinforced with deeds is not likely to be constant.[20]

---

[20] Many students of nonviolence have expressed the belief that it can only be fully understood through practice. See, for example, A. I. Waskow, "Why I Went to Jail" in the *Saturday Review of Literature* 46 (August 24, 1963): 32–33; Joan V. Bondurant, *Conquest of Violence* (Berkeley: University of California Press, 1965), p. 146; and Martin Luther King, Jr., *Stride Toward Freedom* (New York: Harper and Brothers, 1958), p. 101.

Nonviolent activity develops a habit of nonviolence and increases self-discipline. It gives both oneself and others concrete evidence of one's belief and willingness to serve, and it puts inertia on the side of one's continuing to act nonviolently. It might even be said to trap one into continuing to behave nonviolently because one would at least have to contradict oneself, probably have to deny friends, and possibly have to admit error to both the public and one's enemy, if one were to give up nonviolence. This kind of entrapment is worth noting for some of the proponents of nonviolence eloquently denounce entrapment when its effect is to produce violence. They are quite unhappy about the drafting, the training, and the transporting of soldiers who believe, until it is too late, that "it won't happen to me; I will not be killed and I will not have to kill." The soldier is threatened by violence (in the form of imprisonment) if he does not submit to this process of progressive entrapment. With the important difference that they urge every individual voluntarily to involve or entrap himself, proponents of nonviolence seem to desire to set in motion a very similar process, only on behalf of nonviolence rather than violence.

## Questions about Individual Nonviolent Resistance

Several questions concerning the techniques discussed must be explored. First, why does the empathic process cause imitation of nonviolence and not of violence? The answer usually given is that nonviolence holds an advantage because it coincides with reality—with unity. It expresses mankind's communality and is superior in power because it is efficient. It is so because when unity is pursued no energy is expended in maintaining false appearances or in endeavoring to reconcile contradictions between one's conscious and one's unconscious.

Second, can the nonbeliever successfully use nonviolent resistance? To the degree that the success of nonviolence is based on the total integration of the resister's body, mind, will and spirit, it should be clear that nonviolence cannot be successfully practiced by a disbeliever. This is because his hypocrisy would produce inner conflict that would internally consume his energy and thereby diminish the effect he sought to produce. On the other hand, a nonbeliever certainly can behave nonviolently and he may even experience some success while doing so. Many individuals, Martin Luther King, Jr. being perhaps the most famous one, become believers only after participating in nonviolent activity. For this reason nonbelievers are permitted, even encouraged, to try nonviolent resistance. When a demonstration is being organized, participants are usually not asked to make any formal commitment beyond promising to behave nonviolently as long as they are associated with the planned activity.

Third, can nonviolence be successful when directed to immoral or divisive ends, and what would the outcome be if nonviolence were pitted against nonviolence? It seems safe to assume that advocates of individual nonviolent resistance do not believe that it will succeed when directed toward improper goals. They would expect that the "actual truth" (assumed to be possessed by one side) would ultimately triumph, or else that the opposing sides would together arrive at a comprehensive solution. Similarly, when nonviolent techniques are employed by opposing parties, it is assumed that the side genuinely committed to human unity is the one that will win, or else that the two parties will find an inclusive resolution of their differences.

## Mass Individual Nonviolent Resistance

Since the days of Gandhi, theorists of individual nonviolent resistance have been unable to ignore the fact that nonviolent resistance is often collective. Some of them have responded by explaining both individual and group behavior in psychological terms. That is, they describe group action as analogous to individual action, or they refer to a group as though it were nothing more than an aggregate of individuals. For instance, Gregg speaks of the similarities that exist among the behavior of young persons, young movements, and young nations. Also, he speaks of the plight of the world as being due to internationally enlarged, defective individual human relations, and avers that "the law of stimulus and response applies as much to a forest as to a single tree, to the actions of a herd of elephants as to the actions of one elephant." He also describes nonviolent resistance as working by attaching or detaching individuals to or from groups of individuals.[21] Thus, even if group action does occur, it is often described in the same way as individual action is explained.

This lack of differentiation almost precludes any notion of leadership: if absolutely equal people are to act as a group they will have to act either in parallel or in unison. They will individually have to choose to do the same thing or they will have to act according to a unanimity principle. The predictable result of either of these organizing principles is that groups committed to noncoercive, nonviolent activity remain very small, although there may be a large number of these groups.

Usually such a group consists of less than fifteen members. This permits interaction between group members but does not require a hierarchical structure. It increases the receptivity of persons or groups to suggestion and encourages them to conform, but it has as its principal justification that conscious feeling of cohesion and unity toward which all men strive.

Associated resistance can occur in another way: it can be extended not to a large number of people but over a long period of time. In this way one generation can benefit from the behavior and sacrifices of a previous generation. For instance, individual Quakers are today afforded respect and a certain amount of protection because of that sect's long history of nonviolent behavior.

In discussions of individual nonviolence and violence, one finds that emphasis is placed on the *differences* between the two kinds of behavior. However, when the discussion is shifted to group nonviolence and violence, an interesting change occurs: the emphasis is put on the *similarities* between the two kinds of action. Presumably this happens because the advocate of nonviolence wants to

---

[21] Gregg, *Power of Nonviolence,* pp. 64, 117.

argue the undesirability of violence, and to tout the efficiency of nonviolence. Accordingly, at the individual and personal level, at which society usually disapproves of the use of violence, the enthusiast emphasizes how different the two are and how destructive violence is. On the national or international level at which society usually deems violence useful if unpleasant, the advocate stresses how like violence nonviolence is.

Gregg titled one chapter of his book "An Effective Substitute for War"; William James wrote an essay, "The Moral Equivalent of War"; Walter Lippmann, considered "The Political Equivalent of War"; so did Gene Sharp, in "The Political Equivalent of War—Civilian Defense." In each essay the author cogently argues the functional equivalency of nonviolence and of war using the proposition that each fills basic psychological needs ("to live a significant life, to serve a great idea, and sacrifice oneself for a noble cause, to feel the thrill of spiritual unity with one's fellows and to act in accord therewith") and also provides a way of reaching a decision, of settling an issue. Both violent and nonviolent action also require rigorous training, self-discipline, courage, and generosity. They call, too, for the maintenance of a high level of morale, and are predicated on the principle that the way to victory is through the mind, that all struggle is at bottom psychological.[22]

But war and nonviolent resistance are not identical. Although the latter is said to encompass all the virtues of war, it also is said to have positive attributes that war lacks. In particular, it is thought to be more economical than violence. While no one claims that nonviolence will always succeed or that it can succeed without cost, its proponents do believe that it *can* succeed, and that when it does, it does so with less destruction than when violence is used. It is considered a way to save lives, money, and perhaps time.

Such a pragmatic appeal might lead one to suppose that advocates of individual nonviolence consider that it is no more than a ritualized way of conducting an ordinarily violent struggle for power; in other words, that it serves so literally as a substitute for war that it yields precisely the same results violence would have yielded but at a lesser cost. This does not, however, seem to summarize their view adequately. These theorists have such a keen sense of the close relationship between ends and means that it is hard to imagine they would agree that different means could possibly yield precisely the same end. For them, the character of the means used specifically determines the end achieved. The emphasis in individual nonviolent resistance, then, is directed not toward the achieving of a particular goal or toward the seeking of a means to a particular purpose. Instead, it is on the method itself. It is urged because it produces superior results (though not without real cost), not because it produces the same results more economically.

---

[22] William James, *The Moral Equivalent of War* (London: Peace News, 1963). Walter Lippmann, "The Political Equivalent of War," *Atlantic Monthly*, August 1928, pp. 181–87. Gene Sharp, "The Political Equivalent of War—Civilian Defense," *International Conciliation*, no. 555, November 1965. Gregg, *Power of Nonviolence*, pp. 87, 93–95.

## Applied Individual Nonviolent Resistance

Theories deal with abstractions and hypothetical circumstances. The reason for studying them is that they organize knowledge and suggest areas for further inquiry and they predict and thus guide human behavior toward desired ends. Without application, theory is of marginal value, and it is persons like Albert Bigelow, Barbara Deming, and Dorothy Day who have enriched noncoercive nonviolent resistance for us by attempting to practice it systematically. Each of these individuals has pursued a different goal and has adopted different styles and techniques, yet their accounts reflect a common philosophy.

One of Bigelow's adventures has already been discussed. In his book *The Voyage of the Golden Rule,* Bigelow describes the intellectual process underlying his attempts to translate his philosophy into action that would communicate to Americans the "evil" facts about atomic testing. As noted, the method he employed was to try to sail into the Pacific Ocean atomic testing grounds. He planned thereby to risk destruction and to invite arrest; he proposed to move others by voluntarily exposing himself to a penalty. Even though Bigelow and his *Golden Rule* never reached the testing area they did endure governmental harassment, arrest, conviction, and incarceration. They did offer a sacrifice. However, probably because United States authorities did not let them get any further than Hawaii, they did not achieve wide publicity. The struggle was more or less private, and they failed to engage the American public in a significant role. The actions of the U.S. government suggest that it did not want the public involved, so perhaps the public did take part—at least as a potential impartial observer.[23]

In the foreword to his narrative, Bigelow sets forth his cardinal principle, "There are no evil men; only mistaken ones." He also gives expression to his assumption that personality is sacred and mankind unified. Further, he states that his goal is to change men's attitudes without going through a "contest of wills," without "trying to force our opinion on another." Finally, the means employed by Bigelow are like those discussed above: They "appeal to the best in man," by speaking to his reason and conscience, and by his being physically present and prepared to suffer if necessary.

One must wonder at the steady purpose and deliberation with which Bigelow acted in trying to realize his principles. For three weeks after their first detention and conviction, he and his crew remained in Hawaii attempting to reach a unanimous descision as to whether or not they should defy the government and set sail a second time. Interestingly enough, Bigelow was quite critical of his own mission. Believing that "the means come first, not what we accomplish," he was distressed by both his and his crew's impatience, which he regarded as a kind of violence, and by the spirit of the project, which he found "too mental and notional, too speculative and analytical." Bigelow would have preferred more inspiration of the kind that had first suggested the idea of the

---

23 Earle Reynolds, who met and was inspired by Bigelow in Hawaii, *did* sail his ship, the *Phoenix,* into the testing grounds and has also written an account of his voyage and of his inner irresolution. See *The Forbidden Voyage* (New York: D. McKay Co., 1961).

pilgrimage: the kind that came "spontaneously, intuitively from the depths of our beings" and that projected an undertaking that "could not be bypassed, could not be brushed aside, could not be ignored."[24]

Barbara Deming, who has been actively involved in the peace movement and who visited North Vietnam in the spring of 1967, has also eloquently expressed the beliefs underlying the noncoercive nonviolence practiced by individuals. In the sixth portion of her *Prison Notes,* originally published in *Liberation,* Miss Deming describes her experiences as a participant in a Quebec-Washington-Guantanamo Walk for Peace, which inadvertently found itself involved in struggles concerning civil liberties and civil rights issues.[25]

The intention of the peace walkers, who usually numbered between ten and twenty-five, was to walk, and as they walked, to distribute leaflets and to speak before any groups that invited them to do so. They did not propose to stimulate any particular group to any particular action, and the length of their walk was intended to be their chief way of dramatizing their concern. However, as the group entered the southern part of the United States, they found that law enforcement officials interpreted parade and littering ordinances so strictly as sometimes to prohibit absolutely their planned activity. It was also found that the fact that the group was integrated (by chance, not by intention) complicated an already obfuscated discussion of peace and civil liberties with the issue of civil rights.

The group's normal practice was to notify officials in advance of their plans—first, by mail, and second, by an interview with an "advance man." The group was able to "talk its way through" Danville, Virginia, and Americus, Georgia, even though both towns had experienced recent and bitter civil rights struggles. However, in Macon, Georgia, they were arrested. This was in November 1963; the emotional response to the assassination of President John Kennedy brought about their rapid release, however, and not until the next month in Griffin, Georgia, did the group first have its capacity for voluntary suffering put to the test.

In Griffin, the marchers were not only arrested, but they were also subjected to apparently malicious torture by being burned with cattle prods. There, too, devotees of peace were confronted with the problem not of deciding whether or not to merge the peace movement with the civil rights movement, but of deciding whether or not they could possibly be separated. Some decided such a separation was possible and necessary. They left the group stating that they were willing to face death for peace, but that they were "not prepared to die just yet for insisting on my right to walk through the towns of Georgia with Negroes."[26] Others determined to face both issues simultaneously since they had been simultaneously thrust on them.

The site of the next serious confrontation was Albany, Georgia, and

---

[24] Bigelow, *Golden Rule,* pp. 199, 264–67.
[25] The six sections appeared between August 1964 and May 1965. They are also available in a book, *Prison Notes* (New York: Grossman Publishers, 1966).
[26] Dave Dellinger, "Ten Days with the Cuba Walk," *Liberation,* January 1964, pp. 5 ff.

it was in Albany's jail that Miss Deming made her *Notes*. Albany had as its chief of police, Laurie Pritchett, a man who in 1961 had successfully bested a large nonviolent movement led by Martin Luther King, Jr., by using "counter-nonviolence," by enforcing the law strictly but with restraint. Over 1200 persons had been arrested by Pritchett during that struggle, but the resisters were unable to "fill the jails" for officials quickly dispersed them through a number of Southern jails; also, the civil rights organization was thrown into disarray when a third party, the Department of Justice, intervened against them by lodging federal charges against their leaders. Throughout, city officials acted with a minimum of publicity (few outsiders observed the goings-on), and they succeeded in their goals. They made absolutely no concessions, not even the concession of negotiating, or granting recognition.

Albany's confrontation with the peace walkers involved two series of arrests, an "arranged" trial, some forty-nine jail days of solitary confinement, and prolonged and health-threatening fasts. The final result was a "walk," on which five walkers (of various races) were permitted to distribute leaflets over a four-block stretch of the main thoroughfare.

Some nonviolent resistance leaders interpreted these events as "A Victory for Truth," and in doing so noted that the walkers had won exclusively because of their voluntary suffering. Even though the actions of the law enforcement officers had been clearly unlawful, the walkers had not resorted to use of the legal process, since to do so would have been to resort to coercion. Their voluntary suffering was considered especially successful because they managed to involve Albany residents in the issues; the terms for the release of the peace walkers were arranged through negotiations conducted by local white ministers. Finally, the resisters considered their work successful because the concessions they won apparently gave heart to local civil rights leaders. Voter registration pickets appeared on the day of their release. This was the first civil rights activity that had occurred since the devastating defeat of the Albany Movement in 1961.

The conduct of the walkers did not entirely escape criticism, however. A. J. Muste was one of those who was critical of the participants' lack of preparation and concerned by the emotional tensions that existed not only between the resisters and the officials, but within the nonviolent group. Muste also noted "great differences of opinion and some confusion . . . as to why fasting or other practices were engaged in" and warned that "when we make a cult of love for all mankind and find satisfaction in how loving we are, we are probably, in subtle ways, indulging in hate."[27] Both the actions and the cautions described above fit very well with Gregg's views on the proper conduct of nonviolence and with his emphasis on the need for training, rational comprehension, and the avoidance of self-righteousness.

The sixth section of Miss Deming's *Prison Notes* could have been written in direct response to Muste's criticism. (It was actually written to another friend who had expressed sympathy with Miss Deming's goals, but who had questioned the "nonviolentness" of her nonviolence.) In it she denies that to

---

[27] A. J. Muste, "The Meaning of Albany," *Liberation*, April 1964, pp. 18–20.

insist to the point that others feel that they must do violence is to do violence oneself. She also denies that she and her fellows hoped to touch the hearts of their foe "in a very simple and melodramatic way," but asserts that to some extent "one can affect how others will behave simply by looking for one kind of behavior rather than another" (a classic summation of the "self-fulfilling prophecy"). She also seems to refer to what has been called previously cognitive dissonance, when she says that she and her fellow prisoners were able "to bewilder them out of attacking." In speaking of the use of suggestion ("an hypnotic quality"), Miss Deming describes it as being used both on one's opponent and on oneself! She also refers to the need for discipline and to the use of role-playing, in which an actor "trains himself to believe in the events of a play, and through his act of belief he makes the play real." Finally, Miss Deming strongly expresses the need for action. "We believe in the power of nonviolent acts to speak louder than words," she says, for while words are useful to persuasion, action must go one step further and try actually to involve the opponent—if not by capturing his conscience, at least by making him concerned for his image.

Like Bigelow and Miss Deming, Dorothy Day practices what she preaches. Indeed, Miss Day and the Catholic Worker Movement with which she has long been associated probably fulfill the requirements concerning self-discipline and the rendering of service better than any of the other contemporary peace or civil rights groups do.

In *The Long Loneliness* and *Loaves and Fishes,* Miss Day has set forth her own guiding principles: voluntary poverty, manual labor, and love of neighbor. Perhaps there is less emphasis here on active persuasion of others than some would find desirable, but Miss Day's appreciation of just what *love* and *community* mean in terms of everyday living is very sound indeed. She wryly decribes her own attempts to found a communal farm as having ended not in "a community of saints but in a rather slipshod group of individuals." The conscientious, it seems, are contentious, for Miss Day goes on to note that learning to love, practicing love, and paying the cost of love are difficult because individuals do act hatefully and irrationally, lack initiative, talent, or capacity, and sometimes are even violent; but, she continues, the true test of love involves granting forgiveness not to human wrecks who seek help, but to those who routinely work together; not to the utterly forlorn, but to those with whom one lives on an equal and day-to-day basis; not to the ill for whom it is easy to feel sympathy, but to the able-bodied who neglect to help with the dishes.

Miss Day also makes some telling distinctions between "inflicted" and "voluntary" poverty (the second being reversible) and between simplicity and non-ownership (as practiced by members of religious orders); she discusses also "true" poverty which has as its defining characteristic "precarity"—having absolutely nothing in reserve or in store for the future. She further notes that to be truly poor one must live with the poor, share in their suffering, and "give up one's privacy, and mental, and spiritual comforts as well as one's physical."[28]

---

[28] Dorothy Day, *The Long Loneliness* (New York: Harper, 1952), pp. 191, 214; and *Loaves and Fishes* (New York: Harper & Row, 1963), pp. 47, 78, 82, 97.

While proponents of individual nonviolent resistance argue that it is derived from a particular philosophical position, many of them also insist that it is susceptible to scientific explanation. While no one has systematically tried to test or evaluate nonviolence theory as a whole, a number of scholars have investigated or analyzed certain of its aspects. No attempt will be made here to review all the psychological literature relevant to the testing of the tenets of nonviolence. It will be enough to note some of the kinds of studies that have been undertaken.

Professor Jerome Frank, a Johns Hopkins psychiatrist, has written extensively on the subject of nonviolence, and was a primary author of the Group for the Advancement of Psychiatry's (GAP's) report "Psychiatric Aspects of the Prevention of Nuclear War." This study at least partially supports the assumption that there is a fundamental human unity by casting serious doubts on Freud's view that aggression is instinctive and by noting that studies of military behavior have shown that the chief motivation behind the battlefield behavior of soldiers is probably fear and a feeling of group loyalty rather than any need for the release of aggression. The study also points out that soldiers often must be drafted and that in battle they frequently fail to fire their guns in spite of the thorough training given them. While deploring unrealistic mistrust, which is too often self-validating, the GAP authors do not argue that trust is always realistic. They claim only that it is more easily corrected than mistrust is. Also, they make the important observation that trust is something that does not have to be general but can be limited to particular issues. They note, too, that two contending parties can often place trust in a third party even if they are unwilling to trust each other.[29]

The *Journal of Conflict Resolution* regularly publishes reports of experimental work relevant to nonviolence. The work reported there dealing with trust is especially interesting, for it concludes not only that the trusting are trustworthy, but also that those with a common dislike tend to trust each other, and that one who has been trusted is "somehow bound by the trust which is invested in him"[30]—a finding that the advocate of individual nonviolence would clearly expect.

## Conclusion

A coherent account of noncoercive individual nonviolent resistance does seem to exist. Because the individual resister relies on persuasion, he needs access to those who mold policy and opinion, or he requires high visibility, so that he can affect the public as a whole. The likelihood of obtaining both access and visibility are increased if the resister is of high status, but such status is not mandatory.[31] The resister is also more likely to be persuasive if he appeals

---

[29] Group for the Advancement of Psychiatry, *Psychiatric Aspects of the Prevention of Nuclear War* 5, Report no. 57 (September 1964): 230, 234, 289–90, 296–97.

[30] Morton Deutsch, "Trust and Suspicion," *Journal of Conflict Resolution* 2 (December 1958): 265–79.

[31] Jerry Rubin and Abbie Hoffman acquired visibility and status (at least in some circles)

to shared values or to a commonly accepted authority; it also helps to shape one's argument to fit one's opponent's values and his priorities.[32] Persuasion is made easier, too, if the social context in which an individual acts lends him legitimacy: if he is seen as a part of a respected tradition, or if he is associated with a respected institution, especially a church or a religious society. Finally, the chances of success are enhanced if social interaction is based on interdependency and if this interdependency is expected to continue.

Even if individual acts of nonviolent resistance do not fully persuade either government officials or the public, they can fulfill several other useful functions:

1. They can bring new issues into the arena of public discussion.
2. They may change the boundaries of ongoing discussion, for even if the resister does not carry the day he may significantly move the location of "the middle."
3. Nonviolent activity can also give the resister new self-respect and confidence.

The last item is by no means unimportant. The idea that the most positive effect of nonviolence is its effect on the participants themselves has been frequently expressed. No matter what his adversary does, the nonviolent resister can always achieve his own humanity.[33]

This explanation of nonviolent resistance, which is rooted in the writings of Gandhi and in the tradition of the Friends, meets the standards of an explanation in its coherence, consistency, and relevance. It is not, however, *the* explanation of nonviolent resistance. Indeed, examination of the work of Gene Sharp and of others who view the world in terms of groups gives a perspective so different as to be almost polar to this one.

---

through their ingenuity. One of Rubin's first public acts was to testify before the House Un-American Activities Committee dressed as a Revolutionary War soldier. Hoffman threw dollar bills on the floor of the Stock Exchange and conducted an exorcism of the Pentagon. This "monkey warfare" is serious and necessary; it is work, it has required sacrifice, and both Rubin and Hoffman have carried through with what they considered their responsibility.
[32] For instance, even if some one is opposed to integrated schools, he may well prefer open schools to closed schools. The resister's goal, is to arrange things so that he cannot have both, so that he will be forced to choose between them.
[33] This point has had common acceptance by Martin Luther King, Jr., the Quakers, and a present-day psychiatrist. See Stephen Rose, "Test for Nonviolence," *Christian Century* 80 (May 29, 1963): 715; Group for the Advancement of Psychiatry, *Psychiatric Aspects of the Prevention of Nuclear War* 5, Report no. 57 (1964): 297; and Howard H. Brinton, *Guide to Quaker Practice,* Pendle Hill Pamphlets (Wallingford, Pa.: Quaker Center for Religious and Social Study, 1942), p. 56.

# 4  Group Nonviolent Resistance

*Resolve to serve no more, and you are at once freed.*
La Boétie, *Anti-Dictator*

Group nonviolent resistance differs from individual nonviolent resistance in origin, method, and goal. It seems to erupt periodically but spontaneously among populations that have been pushed too far. Such populations tend to use any means available to them, coercive or noncoercive, but they frequently stop short of the use of physical violence. Partly this is because they lack access to effective weapons and partly it is because they fear that the use of violence will produce severe reprisals. The goal of mass resistance is not usually revolution; it is simply amelioration, an improved situation. The resisters do not hope to seize and direct power; they hope only to check it. Also, they do not seek any universal transcendental experience; they do not even imagine one.

In individual nonviolent resistance, intellectual commitment frequently precedes action. One adopts a set of principles and one accepts an explanation; then one deliberately and purposefully acts in a nonviolent and noncoercive manner. In group nonviolent resistance, action is often initiated with little consideration, and frequently little reflection occurs even after all has been said and done. At best, thought comes after the fact; often it does not come at all.[1]

## Assumptions of Group Nonviolent Resistance

Group nonviolent theorists are concerned with the living conditions of groups of people. They do not concern themselves with the individual, his moral purity, or his potential for mystical experience. They neither call, witness, nor testify. Even if they are personally committed to the consistent practice of nonviolence, these theorists rarely refer to their "persuasion." Indeed, they often deliberately dissociate themselves from what is considered traditional pacifism. For instance, they assert specifically and frequently that advocates of group nonviolence

---

[1] One American who has seriously and systematically attempted to formulate an explanation for collective nonviolent resistance is Gene Sharp. His study and analysis have been devoted to improving and increasing the use of such resistance. His goal seems to be one of trying to change the spontaneous to the premeditated. He seems to believe that if unplanned, random, and sporadic mass activity can sometimes be effective, then planned, organized, and sustained activity should be more effective. He hopes that ultimately training in nonviolent resistance will become a part of every citizen's education and that "civilian defense" will be successfully practiced against both foreign invasion and domestic tyranny. Much of the following is drawn from Sharp's work, of which much is yet unpublished and therefore unavailable.

do not have to assume that man is basically good, nor need they assume the existence of a single standard for either truth or morality. They also state unequivocally that the renunciation of violence does not entail servility or passivity. The last point is difficult to establish, but the advocates are clear: to practice nonviolence is not to seek peace at any price. Repose is not their highest purpose; indeed, it is specifically rejected if the price exacted is exploitation or repression—either of themselves or of others.

The group nonviolent resister thinks in terms of society and of the relationships between groups, not in terms of individuals and of their commonality. Also, his commitment is twofold: to social peace and to social justice. He does not let his desire for peace reduce him to abnegation nor does he permit his pursuit of justice to lead him to violence, foreign or domestic. He recognizes that the single-minded pursuit of a single idea often yields nothing but its own antithesis. What he believes his double purpose to require, is a way of fighting for justice that does not produce more injustice than already exists. He offers nonviolent resistance as his solution.

The assumption is that nonviolent resistance is the most economical way to wage struggle, that it minimizes the number of deaths, the suffering of innocents, and the loss of individual freedom. It is not denied that all occur in nonviolent conflict. The only thing that is presumed is that violence would yield more of all three. This is a crucial point. Just as individual nonviolent resistance theory requires one to believe in human unity, group nonviolence theory demands belief in the economy of nonviolence. One accepts it as practical, as realistic, as responsible. One accepts it not as an end, but as a means, and a means to be used on a general rather than restricted basis. It is considered not as one way to manage conflict and not as the way to handle particular kinds of conflict, but as the one and only way to approach all conflict situations.

The third assumption made by theorists of group nonviolent resistance is that conflict not only is real, as opposed to apparent, but also is inherent in social life. This view is in direct contrast to that held by the adherents of individual nonviolent resistance, who believe that conflict is essentially an illusion and one that can and should be dispelled.

Group theorists not only see conflict where others see unity, they find nothing objectionable about it. Indeed, they believe that conflict, whether over values or over claims to status, power, or resources, can be beneficial. They assume and accept conflict whether it is inter- or intra-group, inter- or intra-society, or domestic or international in scope. Among the ways they find conflict useful are the following: They believe, first, it can stimulate intellectual endeavor, which in turn yields new scientific and social ideas; second, it can strengthen the individual's sense of identity and his self-confidence; third, it can increase group cohesion and identity; and fourth, it can serve as an outlet for individual and group hostilities.

In recent years the group conflict model of society has been a dominant model in American political science. Today this pluralist perspective is under attack by some political scientists, who believe that it leads to a justification of the status quo. They argue that to explain society as the product of conflict and to accept conflict as therapeutic is to justify the results of conflict, that is, whatever currently exists. Because they consider justice the only proper social goal, and because they consider it yet elusive, they tend to argue that both the form of conflict and the rules by which it is conducted must be altered.

Group nonviolent resisters would probably concur. In concurring, they probably would not deny that society has worked out a number of very satisfactory "normal" ways of managing conflict. Their point would be only that each has limitations and that even when taken together they do not cover all situations. For instance, efforts to increase understanding are sometimes helpful, but sometimes they cause antagonists to see only too vividly that they have irreconcilable differences they had previously been able to overlook. Similarly compromise, a second way of settling conflict, may be impossible if basic principles are in dispute. Arbitration, a method often used in labor disputes, can proceed only after agreement has been reached as to what party should act as arbiter. Even resort to the democratic process itself does not always put an end to conflict. This is because democracy as majority rule often comes into conflict with the rights of minorities or with the principles of individual freedom. In the same way, plans for world government should not be counted on. Indeed, many nonviolent resisters would note that a world government would continue to be subject to coups d'état, revolutions, and civil war because the fundamental cause of violence is not nationalism but man's faith in violence and his capacity to use it. They argue that it is man's belief in the efficacy of violence that must be obliterated, not conflict, or groups, or nation-states.

Group nonviolent resistance theorists not only believe that conflict is real, they also see its essence as a testing of strength, a pitting of power against power. While these trials may be violent, they need not be. As societies become more and more complex and more and more interdependent, struggle frequently becomes increasingly nonviolent. One reason for this is that as a society becomes more intricate, its forms of power and the ways power can be measured multiply. There are more arenas in which to meet and more devices with which to measure relative strength. A second reason is that while specialization and interdependence increase society's potency, they also increase its vulnerability. In a large and complicated system one can more easily do harm—for example, one person can disrupt a city's power supply or contaminate its water—but at the same time one can more easily be harmed. Thus society develops an interest in tabooing certain kinds of behavior, especially violent behavior. Third, although individual citizens are relatively unarmed, their governments tend to acquire elegant and expensive weaponry. This makes citizens unwilling to challenge their government forcibly and it makes a government more willing to try to control its citizens through persuasion and benefits as opposed to violence, for it looks repressive and weak to use violence when one possesses a preponderance of strength.

Even on the international level, large industrial powers become increasingly reluctant either to challenge each other directly or to test each other by too openly supporting minor powers in their quarrels. Each principal nation fears

escalation, and each realizes that its gains are maximized when combat is restricted to "cold" as opposed to "hot" war techniques. Further, large powers suffer
a public opinion defeat if they use force to control a smaller and weaker country.
Russia and the United States did quiet Czechoslovakia and the Dominican Republic; however, each lost face by doing so. Obviously, major powers do continue to
try to control minor ones, but with subtlety and without violence.

The fact is that violence is not the usual way of testing strength in
modern society. Many methods of measurement now exist and more will be in-
vented. All of those that are nonviolent, the nonviolent resister honors and
accepts; he deprecates none that work. He becomes concerned when no method
works, for his goal is to develop ways of handling intractable issues. His wish is
to eliminate violence even as the weapon of last resort. He would like to do this
by showing that violence is never an adequate way to measure power. Probably
he would settle for demonstrating so many alternative ways of reaching a good
conclusion that one of them would be used and no need to apply violence would
be felt. In short, he would be happy if violence were neglected; he does not
require that it be forsworn as well.

The assumptions discussed here are so different from those made by
the advocates of individual nonviolent resistance that they require review. First,
groups and not individuals are the focus of attention. Second, nonviolent resistance is seen not as the pathway to transcendence, but as a method for conducting
a power struggle that may concern genuinely conflicting interests. Third, its
primary purpose is to demonstrate relative power in a way that is obvious to all
parties and accepted by them but that does not cause lasting damage. If this
cannot be accomplished by changing perceptions, then options are changed. Social
power is reorganized or redirected. Since settlement is reached through a virtual
trial-by-ordeal, it must be clear that coercion and perhaps even the threat of
violence may be an integral part of the process. Still, nonviolence is not necessarily linked to a potential for violence just as all power is not based on violence.[2]

Those liberals and pacifists who ignore or reject the role of power in
social processes cannot effectively practice group nonviolent resistance and they
should not ignorantly advocate it. On the other hand, those who consider
themselves realists should know that nonviolence is sometimes described as war
without violence or struggle without hurt, and they should not be surprised that

---

[2] What seems to be needed is an index for power equivalent to the dollar as a measure of
economic resources. To successfully institutionalize a trial of strength there must be agreement as to how a decision is reached. Violence is most likely to occur when relative strength
is unassessed or differently assessed. For discussion see: Gene Sharp, *The Politics of Nonviolent Action* (Center for International Affairs, Harvard University, August 1966), copy
one, pp. 54, 154; "Functional Equivalent of War," pp. 191–92, 205–06; "Gandhi's Political
Significance for Our Times," in *Gandhi: His Relevance for Our Times*, ed. G. Ramachandran
and T. K. Mahadevan (Bombay: Bharatiya Vidya Bhavan, 1964), p. 54; Lewis A. Coser,
"The Termination of Conflict," *Journal of Conflict Resolution* 5 (December 1961): 347–53;
and Coser, "Peaceful Settlements and the Dysfunctions of Secrecy," *Journal of Conflict
Resolution* 7 (September 1963): 246–53; and Erving Goffman, "Presentation of Self to
Others" in Jerome Manis and Bernard Meltzer, eds., *Symbolic Interaction* (Boston: Allyn and
Bacon, 1967), p. 227.

the work of Sharp is sometimes compared with that of General von Clausewitz. The comparisons between group nonviolence and war differ from those made between individual nonviolence and war, however. They are different in that group nonviolent resistance places emphasis on power and describes nonviolence as a way of ritualizing trials of strength rather than a way to reveal morality. For the group theorist, nonviolence seems genuinely to be a substitute for war, or better, a "functional" (as opposed to dysfunctional) equivalent. That is, it is seen to produce precisely the same results that war would have produced, but at a lower price; its merit is seen not so much in the quality of its outcome as, its accomplishment of war's good purposes while avoiding its bad; it reaches an equivalent decision but with less loss of life.[3] The different courses taken by Ghana and Kenya in seeking their independence after World War II illustrate this point. Both were colonies of England. In Ghana, Kwame Nkrumah led a nonviolent resistance campaign that led to independence in 1957 with little loss of life. In Kenya, Jomo Kenyatta led Mau-Mau terrorists in a murderous campaign that did not drive the English out until 1963 and that cost some 20,000 lives.

## Power and Consent

For individual nonviolent resistance, the fount of power was said to be reality, truth, unity. For group nonviolent resistance, where conflict and change are assumed to be omnipresent and eternal, the nature of power seems somewhat more elusive. Both its manifestations and its sources seem to be multiple. The conventional definition that power is the capacity to control the behavior of others either directly by command or indirectly seems sound but not very concrete, although one can see that nonviolent control could be exercised in a variety of ways, such as authority, persuasion, influence, pressure, coercion, or a combination of these factors.

The thing that must be remembered about group as opposed to individual nonviolent resistance is that all of these instruments fall within its definition of nonviolent action. Any form of power that stops short of physical contact can be considered legitimate, if not wise, according to advocates of group nonviolence. Even though influence, pressure, and coercion refer to methods of eliciting behavior that is decreasingly voluntary, they are not thought to be increasingly offensive. To override another's conscience is considered as permissible as to appeal to it. In short, theorists of individual nonviolent resistance define *nonviolence* very narrowly and then relegate all other forms of control to the category *violent;* in contrast, theorists of group nonviolent resistance define *violence* as destruction or injury to life or property and then call all lesser ways of affecting others *nonviolent.*

In elaborating an explanation of group nonviolence one need not dwell on persuasion, influence, pressure, and coercion. This is because these forms of power are relatively familiar and visible. Careful attention, however, must be

---

[3] Sharp refers to nonviolence as "war itself shorn of many of its ugly features." *Politics of Nonviolent Action,* copy one, p. 171.

paid to "authority," for this form of power is often underappreciated because it is not tangible. Also, authority is not only a *form* of power but also a *source* of power, a source which too often goes unrecognized and is, consequently, under-developed.

Authority is the single most important concept concerning group nonviolent power. It consists of the acceptance by some of another's right to command either because he is thought superior or because he holds an important position or office. Authority always has this dual nature. It always involves both consent (or at least compliance) and command. It is at the same time a source of power and a manifestation of it. It is, in short, power's alpha and its omega.

If authority as command is seen as the primary or at least the most potent form of power, and if authority as consent is seen as the primary or original source of power, then the crux of the nonviolent argument would seem to be that all power ultimately derives from consent. This is precisely the case that is made. The theorist of group nonviolent resistance claims that all governmental power can accurately be said to rest upon consent, even that based on reluctant compliance or that derived from strict enforcement of governmental decrees. This is not just an idle repetition of an old political cliché. It is not just an assertion of what "ought to be." It is considered a literal and a factual description of one of the most fundamental characteristics of all governments; it can be summed up by saying that all rule is permitted by the ruled. Consent is not just a phenomenon of those liberal or communist democracies that describe themselves as servants of the public. It is the foundation of all governments, no matter what rationales they offer for their existence. Some may base their claim on supranational authority, some on a Mandate from Heaven, some on inheritance, and some on the laws of nature. Nevertheless, even when rulers cite these justifications as the basis of their power, what they are actually trying to do is win their subjects' consent.[4]

No ruler's power is derived from his own capacities; it is composed of his capacities plus those of all persons who accept his direction. This means that a ruler's power varies with the number, the talent, and the industry of his subjects. It also means that if a ruler's subjects feel oppressed, they have no one to blame but themselves. It is their own assent that creates their oppressor's power, or as Etienne de la Boétie so nicely put it, in sixteenth-century France: "One's enslaver is oneself," or:

> He who domineers over you has only two eyes, only two
> hands, only one body, no more than is possessed by the
> least man among the infinite numbers dwelling in your
> cities; he has indeed nothing more than the power
> that you confer upon him to destroy you.[5]

Any number of authorities substantiate this view of authority. In addition to La Boétie, there is August Comte: "Authority is derived from

---

[4] Sharp makes this point in *Politics of Nonviolent Action,* copy two, pp. 59–60.
[5] Etienne de la Boétie, *Anti-Dictator* (New York: Columbia University Press, 1942), pp. 11–12.

concurrence, and not concurrence from authority." Then there is Harold Lasswell: "The power relationship is . . . giving and taking. It is cue-giving and cue-taking in a continuing spiral of interaction." Hannah Arendt makes this point both in her essay *On Violence* and in her essay *Civil Disobedience*. Gene Sharp, who has elegantly developed this point, also cites in its support William Godwin, Niccolo Machiavelli, Thomas Hobbes, Leo Tolstoy, Max Weber, Richard Neustadt, Lord Irwin, Karl Deutsch, and Jessie Barnard.[6] The five authors he most frequently refers to as arguing that power is the derivative of consent are T. H. Green, R. M. MacIver, Bertrand de Jouvenal, John Austin, and David Hume. While each of these individuals is an acute political philosopher, none of them can be said to be either an activist or a radical. Nevertheless, it is their work that underpins the arguments for group nonviolent activity, a form of activity that frequently seeks fundamental change.[7]

Proponents of group nonviolence claim that conflict and power are inherent in all social relationships, that conflict is resolved by a test of relative strength, that the essence of power is authority, and that authority rests on consent. Conclusions that follow from these assumptions include the following:

1. Withdrawal of consent or cooperation undermines authority.
2. A decrease in authority leads to a decrease in power.
3. A sufficient decrease in power leads to defeat.
4. Therefore, nonconsent or noncooperation is the most basic weapon available for the waging of struggle.

The quarrel between those who are committed to nonviolence and those who argue that responsible behavior may require the use of violence, then, is not over the latter's assumption that it is sometimes necessary to exercise power, but over their assumption that the use of power requires the use of violence.

If power is derived from consent, nonconsent must result in a decrease in power or its absence. Therefore, the withdrawal of consent might be said to represent a negative form of power. This is because the balance of power clearly is changed in such circumstances; however, the alteration is accomplished through a reduction rather than an augmentation. Nonconsent, then, can be effective, but in a special and negative way. For this reason, victory is precluded, if one means that one gains control and exercises command. What group nonviolent resisters do is veto the actions of others. They do not seize power and carry out

---

[6] Sharp, *Politics of Nonviolent Action*, copy one, pp. 65–73; copy two, pp. 559–64, 568–73.
[7] William A. Gamson argues that governmental power rests not on consent but on trust in *Power and Discontent* (Homewood, Ill.: Dorsey Press, 1968), p. 42. As compared with consent, trust suggests passivity and lack of information. This (or an argument based on compliance) is probably a more accurate way of describing the relationship between the citizen and his government than the consensual presentations of the social contract theorists are. Few have the time or take it to consent actively and intelligently to their government. Gamson also describes a series of experiments designed to see how far people will go in doing disagreeable, nonsensical, and cruel tasks simply because they are told to do so. The degree of trust in authority or compliance with it that was shown (literally) shocked many. Ibid., pp. 127–35.

their own will. For this reason group nonviolent resistance may be radical—that is, it may force fundamental change—but it is not revolutionary. It does not itself seize and then exercise power. Indeed, it might be more useful to refer to group nonviolent resistance as a control of power rather than as a form of power.

Such a description makes nonviolence seem quite palatable. It is hard to portray a nonviolent resister as an enemy of the state when he is not opposed to the exercise of power per se, when he denies any desire to wield power himself, and when he uses a technique that is limited to the limiting of power.

That such a technique is badly needed becomes obvious when one considers the ways in which men have traditionally tried to control each other's power. One method has been to rely on the powerholder's self-control, on something like a code of chivalry, or a privileged individual's sense of noblesse oblige. In relying on such a check, one assumes that every man has his limit as well as his price. One assumes that all men are sufficiently civilized so as to have some standards or some inviolable principles, which no amount of power or temptation will corrode. While it is hard to argue against the importance of thoroughly civilizing all those whom one can reasonably expect to be controlling others' futures, most people are reluctant to rely only on a social code for the control of their rulers.[8]

Because self-control has rarely proved to be sufficiently controlling, men have worked out certain institutions that have as their purpose either the prevention of centralized power or the creation of a counterpower for every existing power. The constitutional arrangements of Western democracies are one example of such check-and-balance institutions. For such devices to be effective, however, men must still exercise self-control, that is, they must abide by the rules. Further, the institutional arrangements must bear some resemblance to the actual distribution of power.

The most obvious way to try to control power is through the exercise of superior power. Unfortunately, there is little reason to suppose that, once victorious, a superior power will control itself, or that any inferior power can hope to control it. This is why so many revolutions go sour. The discipline and control needed to win the revolution do not wither away after power is won, and without an enemy to defeat, the control exercised is felt to be oppressive.

The inadequacy of these methods reinforces the conclusion that non-cooperation, which controls force negatively by reaching to the original source of all power—assent to authority—and cutting it off must be a superior method of control.[9] Perhaps it would be more accurate to say that it is only potentially superior, however, since it is infrequently and inadequately applied.

---

[8] This is especially true because rulers are often told that conventional standards do not apply to them. See Niccolo Machiavelli, *The Prince* (New York: New American Library, 1959), and Max Weber, "Politics as a Vocation," in *From Max Weber: Essays in Sociology,* ed. H. H. Gerth and C. Wright Mills (New York: Oxford University Press, 1958), pp. 77–128.
[9] See Sharp, *Politics of Nonviolent Action,* copy two, pp. 515–19, and also Michael Walzer, "The Idea of Resistance," *Dissent,* Autumn 1960, pp. 369–73.

## Components of Group Nonviolent Resistance

Those who argue the economy of nonviolent resistance are especially concerned that it be put into practice. Gene Sharp has most fully assessed what this would mean, and what the components of nonviolence are. First, he argues, awareness of the possibilities of nonviolent resistance must be created. This awareness, or consciousness, should inform the ruled first that they are ruled, and second that they possess the power to refuse to be ruled. Next the ruler should be made conscious of his incapacity to act alone and of his total dependence on the consent and assistance of others. The creation of such consciousness increases the power of nonviolent resisters by making their previously unrecognized power visible both to them and to their opponent. Their power, which is that of refusing, always exists. However, unless subjects know that it is there, it can go unused; and unless rulers perceive its potency, they may try harsh, although ultimately unsuccessful, repression.

In group nonviolent resistance, what is important is not that individuals perceive truth but that groups understand their potential for power. What is missing today is the people's realization of the crucial role they play in providing the power that is used on them. In part, their ignorance may be due to happenstance, but no authority interested in maximizing his power would reveal this to them, and he would probably try to conceal it. Whether current ignorance is deliberate or not is of little consequence. What is important is that the entire populace learn that their joint or collective resistance can cause a governmental or any other power to disintegrate or dissolve. Even a power that at a particular moment in time may seem invincible should be viewed as vulnerable. Power requires continuously granted consent; thus it is always fragile.

The creation of consciousness obviously calls for a program of education. Because numbers of participants are important in this kind of nonviolence, education obviously cannot be confined to a few devotees who are intensively trained and disciplined, and who then act, at least symbolically, for many others. Instead, the emphasis must be on fundamentals and on mass education. Indeed, the proper place for such training would appear to be the public schools. There future citizens would be taught how to defend their country from foreign invasion without the use of weapons and without leaving home. There they would also learn to resist domestic tyranny, whether the result of usurpation or the product of entirely lawful procedures. If this education were accomplished by courses required both in elementary and in high school, if it were part of every teacher's training, nonviolent resistance might genuinely become a citizen's tool. It might provide the foundation for real participation in government. It might avoid the creation of professional rulers and resisters that now occurs because our division of labor develops specialists and vocationalists instead of amateurs and participants.

Once the power of consent is understood, the next element necessary to its successful use is the will to withhold it. Fear, doubt, self-consciousness, inertia, all these impediments must be overcome. The argument is simple: if one chooses adamantly to refuse, no person and no force can compel one to do anything. Nonviolent strength, therefore, is not so much related to physical capacity as it is to obdurateness or to an indomitable will. If nonviolent resistance fails, then, the fault lies with the actionists. It was they who failed to shed their fear, who lacked sufficient determination, or who did not persist in the face of repression.

Such ringing assertions may be necessary to stimulate action, but brave and strong as they sound, all that is actually being said here is, If one is willing to sacrifice all (including life), or to endure anything (even the worst and long-lasting torture), then one can successfully refuse to comply with any command of any authority. Or, if one has sufficient will, one can always preserve at least one value whatever the external onslaught.

If this were the extent of the message of group nonviolent resistance, one might find it cold comfort indeed. It is not the whole argument but it is important to emphasize the need for strong and enduring commitment, since nonviolent resisters cannot expect their opponents to restrict themselves to nonviolent action. Resisters must be prepared to run real risks and to sustain real casualties. In nonviolent resistance, the "winner" frequently suffers more than the "loser" because he offers his own life instead of trying to take the life of others. Nonviolent resistance can be relatively cheap while being absolutely costly.

Just what is the nature of "will" in a secular theory of resistance? How do education and training strengthen it? Apparently it involves a certainty of purpose—a sureness both as to what ought to be and how it can be brought about. In this context, will does not seem to refer to anything spiritual or mystical; "strong conviction" or "firm belief" would seem to be satisfactory equivalents. The high regard that group resisters have for this inner strength can be shown by their frequently expressed preference for violence over a nonviolence based on cowardice. Generally, the argument is that cowardly nonviolence is the worst possible kind of behavior because it demonstrates both lack of principle and weakness of character. The man who is violent, on the other hand, is assumed to be less fearful and more sure of his goals, even though he may lack self-control or be badly advised. Because he possesses both courage and purpose, the man of violence is considered a more likely convert to nonviolence than the coward. Accordingly, his behavior is preferred.

But maintenance of a steadfast will and demonstration of certainty and self-assurance are not sufficient. Realization of one's purpose, after all, is what matters, and just as it is not enough to have an emotional release of hatred in an act of violence, it is not enough to enjoy a growth of self-respect through the execution of a nonviolent act. To achieve full success, nonviolent resistance usually requires the action to be conscious, highly motivated, and also corporate. The third crucial ingredient, or component, of power is, then, solidarity. Before examining the problems involved in collective behavior, however, it is necessary to examine one more item concerning will.

If one seeks to improve his relative power by refusing to obey and by persuading others not to obey, a study of the factors that cause men to obey would seem to be worthwhile. Sharp and other students of human behavior have contributed some interesting material to the discussion of what creates obedience. Various and multiple reasons for obeying exist, but the most significant seem to be:

1. Habit.
2. Self-interest.
3. Indifference.
4. Lack of self-confidence.
5. Fear.
6. Psychological identification with the ruler.
7. Feeling obliged.

It is not feasible to systematically describe each of these variables and how they relate to each other and to observed behavior. They usually work in combination, although in differing combinations and with varying degrees of significance. Still, the most usual reasons for obeying would seem to be habit, self-interest, and indifference: one obeys reflexively because it is beneficial and/or because one doesn't want to make a fuss. The other causes of compliance seem to come into play when obedience would be in conflict with one's habits or interest, and when compliance *would* make a difference in one's life situation.

"Lack of confidence" would seem to describe individuals suffering from some sort of dissonance or experiencing some kind of cross pressures. These individuals feel tugs from several directions and are unclear as to what ought to be done. Often they resolve their dilemma by following others—by joining the bandwagon.

Sometimes pressure is strong and clear enough that one gives in to it even though it is against one's interest or habit. Then one usually explains his behavior as being based on fear or a feeling of obligation. Conscious fear is probably not a controlling factor in most people's daily behavior. Actions that will produce public vengeance are usually so well defined that one is not tempted to engage in them, and private vengeance is usually either so controlled that one need not fear it, or so sufficiently systematized that one considers it a natural hazard, that is, something to be avoided or suffered but not to be constantly worried about.

Identification with a leader deals with the power of a charismatic personality to lead others even in ways that may not be in their interest. Max Weber provides a thorough discussion of this phenomenon.[10] It seems to require both a very special personality and continued and unblemished success. Because these sets of circumstances are so special, a charismatic leader is more likely to lead a new movement or to have an innovative effect than to build an enduring system that one must resist. Further, because it must always be successful, charismatic leadership is ephemeral, and group nonviolent resisters are usually anxious

---

[10] Max Weber, "The Sociology of Charismatic Authority," in Gerth and Mills, *Essays,* pp. 245–52.

to avoid becoming dependent on it themselves. They prefer decentralized and non-elite leadership. Interestingly and ironically enough, however, nonviolence seems to have had its maximum impact only when it has enjoyed such leadership —only when it has been led by men like Gandhi or Martin Luther King, Jr.

The most frequent cause of obedient behavior that is not in one's self-interest may be peoples' feelings of obligation, their feelings that they should do what they are reluctant to do. Political philosophers tend to write about obligations as though they had objective existence, and moralists tend to assert that people have obligations whether or not they acknowledge them. Even if one does not grant the reality of obligations or the possibility that they can be assigned, it is clear that dutiful feelings affect people's behavior and that individual nonviolent resisters sometimes try to play on these feelings. Group nonviolent resisters are more likely to focus on themselves and the consequences of their acts. Instead of trying to manipulate others' guilt, they concentrate on increasing and wisely using their own capacity. They develop their consciousness to bring their intellectual resources to bear on the struggle at hand, and they strengthen their will so as to mobilize their emotional and unconscious powers. To make their resistance fully effective, only one element is lacking—planned, unified, if you will, conspiratorial action.

To make nay-saying effective, organization is required. Solitary defiance cannot stop repression; widespread defiance can. An individual's refusal to take part in an act of injustice can be converted to an action that actually prevents the injustice if he is part of a group. One cannot emphasize too strongly the importance of collective action. As Hannah Arendt has said: "Power comes into being only if and when men join themselves together for the purpose of action and will disappear when they disperse and desert one another." Power "is simply nonexistent unless it can rely on others."[11] Again, only when resistance is so general that the ruler can find no one to commit unjust acts for him does nonviolence become maximally effective, and only in these limited circumstances could one possibly describe nonviolence as being a positive form of power.

Two important problems remain for the nonviolent activist: one is how to inspire large numbers of individuals to face the possibility of martyrdom, and the other is how most effectively to organize their resistance without having recourse to the use of violence. The achievement of these goals requires a knowledge of society's organization.

## Hierarchy and Nonviolent Power

The proposition that oppression is, at bottom, the result of voluntary acceptance, appears to structure conflict as either a one-to-one struggle between ruler and resister, or as an opposition between a single ruler and his collective subjects. Any "power structure," however, is complex; there exist varying degrees of responsibility for any action taken, of enthusiasm for participation, as

---

[11] Sharp, "Freedom and Revolution," review of *On Revolution* by Hannah Arendt, in *Peace News,* February 14, 1964, p. 8.

well as varying costs paid for deviant behavior. Still, any wise ruler makes an effort to have a rebellious subject feel that he is "but one," while the government is "at one" with the rest of society. Similarly, any advocate of resistance will emphasize the oneness of the ruler as contrasted to the collectivity—potential if not actual—of the resisters. These practical considerations may well account for the oversimplified view of society presented in much resistance literature.

Anyone who seriously addresses himself to the effective conduct of resistance must deal with an intricate social structure. He must consider, at a minimum, the elite, their functionaries, and the masses. The elite include the rulers, the policymakers, and the leaders, in a wide variety of fields both in and out of government. The functionaries are the executors; they are the soldiers, the law officers, the tax collectors, the teachers, all those upon whom the system relies to control and direct each other and the rest of the population or the mass.

Often elites are relatively immune to moral appeals because their positions of leadership have accustomed them to compartmentalize their moral and governing identities. They know they are not like others, and they assume that their moral obligations are different from those of ordinary men. Further, resisters rarely have access to elites; therefore they have no opportunity of making a moral appeal. Further, elites do not have to carry out their own policies; they order "protective-reaction strikes," but they do not personally bomb civilians.

If the resister influences a society's functionaries, he influences those on whom the elite depends. To challenge the apparatus rather than the elite itself is not, however, to confront a weak point in one's opposition. The allegiance of these subordinates is not usually based on an unstable emotion like fear, but is rooted in more constant feelings such as identification with the rulers, obligation to them, perceived self-interest, and/or habit. Still, it is the administrative level that actually confronts the resisters and determines whether or not they will succeed. Whether functionaries do or do not share the values of the resisters is of little consequence. Their behavior is what counts, and what is important is that the functionaries do not have to join the resisters in order to assist them. It is enough if they fail to fulfill their function. Disenchanted intellectuals may begin a revolution, but its culmination comes when tax collectors don't collect, police don't arrest, and soldiers don't shoot.[12]

The resisters must also try to predict how nonparticipants will react to their challenge, whether they will remain uninvolved, whether they will serve as impartial observers, whether they will function as an approving audience, or whether they will actually become allies.

As to the uninvolved, sometimes one only tries to keep them that way. In Central America, for instance, a resister typically hopes the United States government will not intervene. Yet the role of the audience can be crucial. One may seek impartiality when he is sure he is right, but a resister usually hopes this will lead to an openly supportive audience. Northerners have often argued that

---

[12] See D. J. Goodspeed, *The Conspirators: A Study of the Coup d'Etat* (New York: Viking Press, 1962), chap. 7.

the Ku Klux Klan acted as it did because upper-class Southerners condoned its actions although they did not participate in them. Similarly, nonviolent resisters often hold demonstrations in which only a limited number of persons offer resistance such as refusing military induction, but in which many offer applause.[13] Supporters may be one of two kinds. They may have the same specific goal as the resisters but different resources and risks (an example would be white liberals committed to black civil rights), or they may have different goals but feel they have a common enemy (an example might be those seeking legalization of marijuana, those seeking the end of the draft, and women liberationists).

The chief characteristic of the masses is their lack of organization. Their behavior tends to swing between apathy and nondirected, chaotic agitation. The group resister must inspire and organize them.

First the activist must decide what kind of organization will best promote successful resistance. Most group nonviolent theorists emphasize two principles: solidarity and decentralization. Solidarity involves both number and cohesion. Number is important because the chances of any one person's being punished are reduced when he acts in concert with a large number of others. A second reason is that the more resisters, the fewer available to enforce the ruler's will. A third reason is that a large number of resisters lends credibility to a position, both because it demonstrates power or potential power and because the rightness of a position is often thought to relate to the number of persons taking it.

It is important that the resistance leaders and their cadres mobilize, discipline, and direct as many of the mass as possible. It is also important that this not be too centrally organized. If it is, the leaders can be made ineffective through legal harassment even if they are never found guilty of a crime. There must be many leaders and many organizations available; power must be diffused. Even the best of leaders represents a threat to his organization if he is its sole source of authority because an outsider or a usurper can destroy an organization or gain full control over it simply by striking and overwhelming the single site of power. The Greek coup d'état of 1967 illustrates well the dangers inherent in overcentralization. In this case the government of Greece was not ordinarily highly centralized. However, there was in existence a plan for concentrating governmental power in the event of a national emergency, and there also was an easily invoked routine for proclaiming such an emergency. Thus, the task of the conspirators was easy. Once they had put the emergency plan into opera-

---

[13] The importance of audience sanction should not be underestimated. Mayor Richard Daley indicated clear support of violent law enforcement during Chicago's racial disturbances in 1967, and police violence escalated after that. A high Ohio official publicly condoned rigorous law enforcement just before the Kent State slayings. And Governor Ronald Reagan of California indicated his belief that a "bloodbath" might be necessary shortly before a student was shot (accidentally, but by officials) at the University of California at Santa Barbara. For discussion see Arthur I. Waskow, *From Race Riot to Sit-In* (Garden City, N.Y.: Doubleday & Co., 1966); and Waskow, "How to Avoid a Race Riot," *Saturday Review* 46 (July 6, 1963): 8 ff.; and William A. Westley, "The Escalation of Violence through Legitimization," in *Patterns of Violence. Annals of the American Academy of Political and Social Science*, ed. Marvin Wolfgang, 364 (Philadelphia: March 1966): 120–26.

tion they could seize all power by seizing only a few command posts, and this is exactly what they did.

For the nonviolent resister, the ideal social structure seems to be one that is highly cohesive but that lacks hierarchical organization. The phrase "decentralized solidarity" would seem an accurate, if paradoxical, description of this situation. Unfortunately this kind of social structure usually requires several special circumstances. First, cohesion requires argeement: it suggests homogeneity or similarity. On the other hand, lack of hierarchy requires simplicity, lack of complexity, lack of differentiation. What seems to be suggested is a rustic, egalitarian kind of society of a type that was outdated even when it was advocated by Jean-Jacques Rousseau.

Some present-day political theorists argue, however, that solidarity can exist even in a technological society, and that a heterogeneous society is capable of acting collectively. Clearly a society does so in the name of nationhood; it also seems to do so when challenged by an alien ideology. What seems to be required is a set of common values, or more likely, an agreed-upon way of conducting business. Thus, agreement on procedure may work as well as agreement on purposes, or even better. Further, agreement may not have to be positive; a collective response does not have to focus on what people are for; it can as easily be organized around what they are against. All can agree to avoid hell even if they cannot agree on a definition of heaven.

Decentralization does not have to mean lack of central direction, nor does it have to mean lack of hierarchical organization. It can mean that there is a wide distribution not of power and leadership but of potential power and leadership. What is required is rotating, or at least rotatable, leadership with a widely distributed veto power. This could be accomplished by widely distributing the weapons of nonviolent resistance: mimeographs, radio sets, cars, even food supplies. The goal of this strategy would be to give each citizen some capacity to defend himself but to ensure that none would have the capacity to control others. At the same time, official power can be deliberately made vulnerable. Strict prohibitions against secrecy could be enforced so that citizens would know the precise identity and physical location of all individuals they wished to question or challenge or of files they wished to inspect. Enforcement and intelligence agencies could be staffed by short-term draftees or even by volunteers instead of professionals. Similarly, taxes could be made voluntary, or at least could be annually paid by the citizen and not withheld by the government. Contrived and inconvenient as these rules or devices may seem, their intent is to ensure responsive government by deliberately giving the people power. Their purpose is to make individual rights such as free speech meaningful. In this case by ensuring (1) that the speech is heard, and (2) that it is considered, if for no other reason than because of what may happen if it is not. The fact that potential power is conscientiously distributed does not mean that it must or will be exercised. It does not create equality; it should, however, increase citizen efficacy.

The traditional way of trying to achieve the special kind of solidarity that integrates a community and at the same time emphasizes decentralization and individual self-sufficiency is through participation. Participation is seen as the way to synthesize collective action and individual freedom, as a way one can continuously express his consent to governmental power. In our representative democracy, one usually expresses his consent only periodically and only in a limited way: only on election days and only by choosing between several pre-selected candidates.

The difficulty with justifying power on the basis of this kind of participation is that no real provision is made for the expression of nonconsent. Advocates of nonviolent resistance do argue that of course nonconsent can be expressed by nonparticipation, and that it can be effective if there are many determined nonparticipants. Nevertheless it is still true that ever since the days of John Locke simple nonparticipation has been construed not as nonconsent but as consent. Inertia has been placed squarely on the side of authority. What seems to be needed is a way of registering nonconsent, of withdrawing from the state and becoming a neutral rather than either an outlaw or an enemy. The logical conclusion of a consent argument should be that one chooses his citizenship instead of having it associated with his geographical location. Laws would then apply to those persons who consented to membership in a political body and not to every single person residing within certain geographical boundaries.[14]

Even resisters who consider participation in a representative democracy to be a sham do not underestimate the importance of genuine participation. Therefore, just as individual resisters emphasize the importance of action to commitment, group resisters emphasize the need for participation to enhance solidarity. They recognize that belonging to a group and working with it increases the individual's feelings of responsibility, of courage, and of capacity, and that his commitment to the whole or to the future makes him more willing to sacrifice. Those who organize resistance, therefore, try to focus on a set of agreed-upon goals, try to create a group identity through high interaction and the use of symbols, and seek recognition by others of their group's identity.

Analysis of a society's structure must include consideration of all its components, even though only a part of them are consciously and actively involved in any particular conflict. Also, one must expect that most people will consider themselves uninvolved, even those who are being challenged! Third, while resisters may attempt to directly confront their opponent and his supporters, they may also follow strategies of involving the uninvolved, or of mobilizing the unmobilized. Fourth, any strategy rooted in social organization must be an ever-changing strategy, because such organization is dynamic rather

---

[14] At one time in Europe, individuals who lived in close association with one another were subject to a number of different tribal and religious laws. Perhaps in the "global village" of the future, individuals will be able to choose their tribe and law, and "parallel institutions" will everywhere coexist. Homosexuals will not have to threaten to take over Alpine, California, and blacks will not argue that their protection requires that they be given Mississippi, Alabama, Georgia, and Louisiana.

than static. At any single moment, one's opponent may appear invulnerable. However, his interests, his resources, and his allies are always changing and a resister should rarely conclude that his goals are permanently unrealizable.

## Techniques of Group Nonviolent Resistance

Collective nonviolent techniques are aimed at altering power relationships. They seek to increase the resisters' consciousness, will, solidarity, and number and/or to decrease their opponent's conciousness, will, solidarity, and number.

Since human relationships are predicated on cooperation, denial of cooperation can be an effective way of exercising power. Withdrawal of support, or of consent, can take an infinite number of forms and can be practiced by any number of people. If the resisters are few, their positions unimportant, or their recalcitrance brief, their nonconsent can be described as protest, as a form of expression.

Often protest is not consciously associated with power. Indeed, the contrary is often assumed, since a protester often appears to be losing or to have lost his battle. However, the vigor with which different societies suppress different kinds of dissent makes it quite clear that protest can be perceived as very threatening. It is almost as though authorities fear that someone will point out that they do not, like the emperor, have any clothes on![15] Protest is also often thought not to involve much in the way of discipline or sacrifice, but even thoroughly legal protest can exact a high price. It can mean loss of employment, broken friendships, and public ridicule. Still, while its costs are real, they are rarely mortal.

On occasion protest may convert an opponent. However, because the essence of protest is psychologically to attack one's opponent, or at least to put him on the defensive, protest does not usually change his mind—at least not at once and not directly. Long-term and indirect effects are a different and important matter, however. The Gallup Poll shows that American public opinion reversed itself on the subject of the Vietnam War in a period of three or four years. This reversal correlated with a great deal of antiwar protest.[16] Yet one cannot prove a cause-and-effect relationship between the two. Individuals who admit that they have changed their minds often specifically deny that protest has had any effect on their thinking. Perhaps the power that protest demonstrates can best be described as symbolic, or perhaps as prefiguring.

---

[15] See Hans Christian Andersen, *The Emperor's New Clothes,* in any of many editions.
[16] The anti-Vietnam War movement has demonstrated a particular flair for imaginative protest. It has marched with flowers and flags to guitar music, it has staged mock funerals and guerrilla raids, and it has sponsored Vietnam veterans in a protest ceremony featuring the return of military decorations. The potency such protest can have is shown by the vigor of the response made by Mayor Richard Daley's Chicago police force. Similarly, former Attorney General John Mitchell's decision to prosecute seven protest leaders for conspiracy also indicates the seriousness with which scornful rejection of government policy is viewed. Finally, the Chicago Seven's use of their trial as a stage demonstrates not only their contempt but their belief that "the best sabotage is sabotage that destroys the society's magic," in this case, respect for judicial authority. See Jerry Rubin, *We Are Everywhere* (New York: Harper & Row, 1971), p. 150.

Sometimes protest actually diminishes one's power. This happens when the protester uses it primarily as a form of self-expression, when he registers his dissent and then feels relieved of any further responsibility. The resister's activity then ceases; he enjoys a catharsis; he does not really care whether or not his protest has also acted as a catalyst.

Group protesters usually seek widespread visibility rather than intimate access. Today this means coverage by network news and the wire services. Even if these concentrated media do not control how the American public thinks, they do exercise another subtle form of power, that of controlling what the public thinks about. They set the agenda even if they do not determine outcomes.[17] Protesters must exercise much ingenuity and expertise to obtain valuable media attention. In contrast, the President and a number of other government officials can virtually command coverage; also, officials can sometimes delay or even black out stories about protest activity.[18] A further difficulty involves the fact that protesters cannot expect that the message they send will necessarily be the one received. Different people interpret the same event differently. Many Americans believed they had witnessed a police riot during the 1968 Democratic convention in Chicago. A greater number of Americans believed they had seen a hippie riot and one that was quite properly quashed.

What specific techniques are suitable for protest activity? Many are obvious: the writing of letters, the signing of petitions, the running of ads, the wearing of buttons, and the sporting of bumper stickers. Others are more dramatic: the holding of mock trials, emigration, renunciation of citizenship, the "haunting" of public officials,[19] public disrobing, and even destruction of one's property or of one's self. The fundamental goal is communication; the means are myriad.

Nonviolent action becomes more than expressive when normal social relationships are disrupted. Disruption that derives from withdrawn cooperation or refused assistance may be described as *resistance*. This may occur in any of a number of spheres—social, economic, or political.

Social snubs, sexual noncooperation à la Lysistrata, even emigration are all forms of social noncooperation. There are the fundamental techniques of economic noncooperation, the boycott and the strike. The boycott may be by consumers, producers, bank depositors, renters, even international tourists or traders. A strike can involve any group of workers and may be directed at a single employer or at a whole industry; it may seek particular goals or may serve as an expression of sympathy; it may be a general strike or an exceedingly limited one; it may be one of long duration or it may be a quickie; it may be a slow-

---

[17] The power involved in deciding what issues are addressed is discussed in Peter Bachrach and Morton Baratz, "The Two Faces of Power," *American Political Science Review* 56 (1962): 947–52.

[18] See, for example, Merrill Proudfoot, *Diary of a Sit-In* (Chapel Hill: University of North Carolina Press, 1962), p. 7.

[19] One of the original devices used by the Oakland Black Panthers was "policing the police as they carried out their duties in ghetto areas. This created much attention; it did not improve relations between the Panthers and the police.

down strike or a selective one. The variations are almost infinite, but the method chosen always seeks to maximize one's relative power. Techniques of political noncooperation involve refusal to take oaths or to give public endorsement, slow compliance, boycott of elections or of government employment, tax refusal, civil disobedience, even the building of alternative institutions. Political noncooperation may be legal, illegal, or extralegal. It may involve behavior that is normally voluntary or normally required.

It is difficult to generalize as to whether noncooperative acts should be considered persuasive or coercive in intent. Generally their effect on the opponent depends on the number of resisters and their location in the social structure. For instance, a strike by short-order cooks would have more impact than one by furriers. A strike by 5,000 New York City policemen would be more effective than one by 5,000 policemen scattered randomly over the country. A strike by all news wire services would be felt more than one by all FBI agents. So technique, or the nature of an act, does not in itself determine whether that act's effect is emotionally or rationally to appeal to another's better self, or whether its effect is to limit his field of action or even to jeopardize his well-being.

Usually noncooperation assumes previous cooperation. Withdrawal results in inconvenience if not actual distress. However, every society has persons or groups that it prefers to ignore if not to exclude. These people are cooperating with the dominant society if they withdraw from it! To noncooperate with a society that rejects them, these people must insist on interaction.

To insist upon interacting with someone who does not desire contact can be called intervention. When it is described as intervention instead of as a special kind of noncooperation, one can understand why this kind of nonviolent activity is often controversial. Even though its effect on public opinion is potent, it is not always predictable. In 1971, traffic was deliberately and severely disrupted in Washington, D.C., in May and in New York in June. In the first instance, Mayday demonstrators intervened in the flow of traffic—often by standing in the street. The government's response has already been discussed. It included among other things illegal mass arrests which the President of the United States tried to justify on national television. In New York, the traffic disruption was caused by drawbridge operators who opened their bridges, locked them, and went home. Here no reprisals were taken; the President did not even comment.

In part, the different responses to two deliberate disruptions of traffic was due to one act's being interpreted as intervention and the other as noncooperation; one was viewed as a sin of commission, the other as one of omission. The former is almost always thought of as more serious. Perhaps because it is clearer—there is no doubt about its intent. Perhaps, too, it is because the asocial behavior of established members of society is most often a result of their failure to act, they being the ones who have the capacity to do so, while the lower strata, lacking capacity, cannot be asocial by failing to act. Their misdeeds are almost necessarily ones of commission rather than omission.[20]

---

[20] Another important difference was that organized labor was involved in the second traffic

Intervention involves the doing of unusual acts. The aim is to obstruct another's acts or at least to force him to take notice of a particular situation by physically or psychologically intruding oneself. Psychological interjection can be accomplished through such devices as fasting; implementing a reverse strike, in which one does what the government has not done, for instance, cleaning up a park, working overtime to accomplish the day's work, or privately providing what should be public services; and seeking imprisonment. Physical intervention can take the form of the "ins"—sit, stall, ride, or wade—or it could involve the overloading of social facilities or the actual invasion of buildings and offices.

Acts of nonviolent intervention, like those of noncooperation, cannot be classified per se as either persuasive or coercive. However, because of the tendency for acts of commission to be perceived as more aggressive than those of omission they are usually held to be coercive. Most advocates of collective nonviolent resistance make no moral distinction between persuasive and coercive action; nor do they distinguish protest, resistance, or intervention on moral grounds; they do not even suggest that these types of action should be used sequentially. Indeed, most of them seem to believe that one can work for non-violent conversion and coercion simultaneously, and also that nonviolent action can be used in conjunction with conventional educational and political techniques. Their purpose in studying technique and in compiling exhaustive lists of non-violent activities is not to establish any order of moral preference, but to make available a body of raw data for further analysis and to provide a checklist of possibilities for action.

## Applied Group Nonviolent Resistance

In a monograph published by *Peace News* and entitled *Tyranny Could Not Quell Them,* Sharp has analyzed the collective resistance of Norwegian school teachers to Nazi attempts to reorganize the Norwegian national school system during World War II. This interesting case study shows the importance of society's structure and also serves as a paradigm of how collective nonviolent resistance could optimally develop.

In this case, the original nonviolent resistance arose because of an attempt by the Germans to organize a new teachers' organization devoted to Nazi principles. This meant that the Norwegian teachers had two reasons for resisting. The first was to assert their own nationality; the second was to preserve the integrity of their collective high-status profession. The teachers' first act of resistance entailed nothing more than the sending of a letter that stated that membership in the new group appeared to be in conflict with the fundamental obligations of the teaching profession. Approximately three-fourths of Norway's teachers sent such letters, in an act that seems to have been as spontaneous as any human event ever is. Each letter was the work of an individual—that is, the letters

---

disruption, and in the U.S. today society expects and tolerates dislocations caused by workers seeking to improve their lot. This toleration is of recent vintage and it was hard won. New groups may win a similar "right to disrupt," but they must expect to pay for it first.

were not collected and sent as a group. In addition, the action was taken without the benefit of known leadership. In describing the organization, Sharp quotes participants as saying, "We never knew from whom the orders came. . . . They were obeyed because they came through people who had put themselves in charge." Sharp then goes on to narrate in detail the events that followed this initial refusal. One thousand (of eight thousand) randomly selected teachers were arrested; of these 650 were sent to a northern concentration camp. Even in prison the teachers resisted the Nazi demands. Finally the Germans relented. Six months later the teachers were released and returned to their original positions.

Sharp regards this as a model exercise. At the same time he is aware that much of its success was due to circumstance rather than to intelligence, moral strength, or calculated solidarity. First, the teachers belonged to a group that was of manageable size, high status, and easily identifiable. It was, moreover, committed to a set of principles; its primary goal was neither economic nor the exercise of power. In this way, the teachers were like the Norwegian clergy, who also successfully resisted the Nazis; they were unlike the labor union members and the politicians, who were not so successful in their resistance. Further, their challenge was to an invading power and to its proposed changes. Thus, both nationalism and inertia worked to the teachers' benefit. Also, the initial action required of the teachers was simple. It was to state their intention not to take an action. Having made this minimal commitment, the resisters then relinquished the initiative to the Nazis. The Germans did make arrests, they did subject the prisoners to discomfort (inadequate food, strenuous calisthenics, and exile to the north) but they did not practice torture or random execution, and most important, once the exile had begun, the Nazis did not give the prisoners an opportunity individually to recant; thus they aided them in the maintenance of their solidarity. In addition, knowing that other Norwegians were suffering severely from the war probably made the teachers better able to bear their own burden. All these items made resistance easier. All this Sharp admits; he even quotes one teacher as saying, "In many ways our victory was organized by the enemy." Nevertheless, Sharp makes an important point: that many circumstances like those that spontaneously occurred in this instance might be planned for and arranged to occur in the future. It is Sharp's argument that nonviolent resistance, or "unarmed defense," can and should be consciously prepared for. He argues especially the need (1) to create a society that commands the loyalty of its citizens as fully as the teachers' profession did; (2) to encourage self-reliance and also the development of a number of independent organizations and communications networks; and (3) to organize formal study and teaching of techniques of nonviolence such as were practiced spontaneously in this case.[21]

---

[21] Krishnalal Shridharani, *War Without Violence* (Bombay: Bharatiya Vidya Bhavan, 1962) discusses similar matters. This volume is the product of five years of participation in Gandhi's resistance campaigns and a Columbia University Ph.D. The subject as Shridharani defines it is *Satyagraha,* a form of nonviolent resistance that consists of five stages: negotiation, agitation, demonstration, self-purification, and direct action. While Sharp does not place much emphasis on temporal sequence, Shridharani's stages correspond almost exactly with the vital elements of Sharp's discussion.

By first attempting negotiation, the resister satisfies himself and demonstrates to

Finally, James Farmer, once the National Director of the Congress of Racial Equality, articulates an applied collective view of nonviolence in his book *Freedom—When?* Farmer, who considers himself a student of Gandhi, notes that nonviolence has "more in common with war than with pacifism," and he refers to its advocates as soldiers, not as disciples. Other points he emphasizes that are important to an understanding of group nonviolent resistance include the following: first, that change does not occur easily—it involves both tension and "creative conflict," which often become intense just before change is effected; second, that "love is a luxurious tactic" when changes in specific behavior and particular conditions can be achieved simply by making them "unfeasibly expensive and inconvenient;" third, that while the resister is responsible for his own conduct, he does not bear the responsibility for the hatred and brutality manifested by his opponent in a period of tension, nor is he responsible for provoking the noninvolved public if the mass media have not accurately reported events and the context in which they occur; fourth, and finally, that nonviolence is a weapon—one that has "tested out and proven effective." Thus, Farmer concludes that nonviolence is more than a philosophy or an idealism that can end in irrelevancy or in "whispering through an occasional keyhole to another human heart"; he believes also that it is more than a safe way of expressing an anger that ends in nihilism. To him it is a strategy, one that encompasses "prudence, tactical good sense, and our ideals."[22]

## Conclusion

It can now be seen that the group approach to nonviolent resistance is quite different from the individual approach. It begins by assuming that life is filled with conflicts in which groups of men test and try each other. The outcome of these struggles is thought to be determined by superior power. The reason for adhering to nonviolence in these contests is not to put an end to struggle and the exercise of power, but to make struggle as nondestructive as possible. Little use is made of moral argument, for the crucial point is economical: that a nonviolent trial is the cheapest way to measure relative power. Usually, the argument is cast positively rather than negatively. There is little lamentation, and there are few recriminations; instead, the emphasis is on the intelligent development of power through deliberate, disciplined, collective action.[23]

---

others that the authorities are unresponsive and that ordinary channels for conflict resolution are inadequate. This is a state of affairs that Shridharani assumes will recur periodically because no political system is capable of achieving sufficient change by strictly legal means. Shridharani's second stage, agitation, seems to correspond with Sharp's discussion of the creation of consciousness. The third stage, demonstration, lends color and drama to one's cause and is intended to create social contagion, or as Sharp would have it, solidarity. Self-purification is clearly intended to strengthen one's will. (The particular flaw one must purge according to Shridharani, is that of having submitted, or having consented to one's own debasement.) Finally, direct action for Shridharani, like Sharp, refers to a wide range of noncoercive and coercive activities that may be undertaken to determine the "relative strength of the people" (p. 286).

[22] James Farmer, *Freedom—When?* (New York: Random House, 1965), pp. 55, 73, 82, 70, 72, 33, 37, 82.

[23] In recent years, several community organizers have tried to instruct others in the develop-

Nonviolent power is considered uniquely safe as well as uniquely economical; nonviolent resisters rarely move on from the successful defense of their own way of life to active control over the lives of others. This is because there are certain checks inherent in nonviolent resistance. First, the resister does not threaten others with violence but, on the contrary, risks violence against himself; by doing this he "guarantees" his sincerity (as Joan Bondurant says). Second, even those nonviolent resisters who allow or invite third parties to use threats or violence on their behalf or who have recourse to legal proceedings automatically set a limit on their action. They obtain only what others will win for them, and this is a limit because customarily the limits of the altruistic behavior of third parties are reached more quickly than those of the egoistic behavior of resisters. Third, the strength of will and group solidarity necessary to wage nonviolent resistance seems to be maximized when one is in opposition. That is, it seems to be injustice (about which men can often agree) rather than justice (about which men can rarely agree) that stimulates inspired action. Thus, group solidarity seems to rest on the "comradeship of common jeopardy" or to consist of a "fellowship of sufferers" more often than it focuses on a group's positive beliefs or experiences.[24] These points seem to support what is a strong presumption in discussions of nonviolent resistance—the argument that privilege cannot be protected nonviolently. This point both justifies such resistance and sets a limit on it. Again, the reasoning is that an individual will not risk high stakes for something he regards as a luxury rather than as a necessity; that while third parties may sacrifice to defend other people's deserts, they will not defend other people's privileges; that people can agree on what is wrong more easily than on what is right; and perhaps, that because privilege is associated with a minority it will be difficult to defend it against an aroused majority. Tolstoy's observation seems acute: "The question of Non-Resistance to [violent evil] seems to them [the privileged] an astonishing absurdity, and the more absurd, the more advantages they enjoy under the present system."[25]

Advocates of group nonviolent resistance urge its use even in the one area where most people find it most unrealistic—in the realm of foreign affairs. Resisters do this partly out of an appreciation of the horror nuclear conflict could unleash, but also because they believe nationalism is one of the few

---

ment of community power. Saul Alinsky has offered *Reveille for Radicals* (New York: Random House, 1969) and *Rules for Revolution* (New York: Random House, 1970). Also, excellent step-by-step manuals have been prepared by Charles Walker, *Organizing for Nonviolent Direct Action* (Cheney, Pa.: by the author, 1961), and by Martin Oppenheimer and George Lakey, *A Manual for Direct Action* (Chicago: Quadrangle Books, 1964). The last has excellent chapters on analyzing power in a community, establishing a nonviolent organization, conducting actual resistance, and protecting oneself against private and/or governmental retaliation.

24 See Merrill Proudfoot, *Diary of a Sit-In* (Chapel Hill: University of North Carolina Press, 1962), p. 37; Howard Thurman, *Luminous Darkness* (New York: Harper & Row, 1965), p. 55; and Clarence Case, *Nonviolent Coercion* (New York: Century Co., 1923), pp. 406–13.

25 Leo Tolstoy, *The Law of Violence and the Law of Love* (London: Westminster Press, 1959), p. 98.

forces capable of creating a truly viable solidarity. While group resisters argue that they do not need to share the values of their opponent, they are quite clear about the fact that the resisters must possess strong bonds with one another. Since nationalism has so often proven a stronger bond than class, or race, or ideology, it may actually (and perhaps ironically) be that nonviolent resistance has a greater potential for success in international conflict than in domestic conflict.

One advantage it has is that it utilizes the whole population. Traditionally civilians have been expected to support the military in its operations, but for the most part, they have been expected safely to await at home the verdict rendered on the battlefield. Unfortunately, in many situations today civilians are not permitted the luxury of noninvolvement. In totalitarian states they are players of assigned roles; in guerrilla warfare they are willing or unwilling participants; in nuclear warfare they are collective victims. Thus, because one is involved willy-nilly, it seems reasonable to defend oneself as best one can. Because civilians are selected out as being those least fit for conventional warfare, or for the waging of violent struggle, it seems obvious that they should concern themselves with organizing the power that is available to them, and it also seems obvious that the power that they can best use is nonviolent in nature.[26]

Sharp has called the activities in which the less fit can engage by the name civilian defense. It is a kind of defense that has little in common with what the United States government now calls civil defense. The latter focuses on evacuating target areas, hiding in bomb shelters, and rendering first aid. It is passive. In contrast, civilian defense is active. It works to educate and train citizens to use power, a power that is not derived from arms or from a coercively organized collective force, but rather that nonviolent, noncooperative power that comes from conscious preparation, will, and voluntary solidarity.

In theory, civilian power would be widely dispersed; it would be organized through nongovernmental groups such as unions, churches, and schools in such a way that "micro-resistance" would "honeycomb" the nation.[27] In theory, too, an organized civilian defense network would render international service in times of emergency. Volunteers would assist those stricken by flood, fire, earthquake, or disease. This would be intrinsically beneficial, it would create favorable world opinion, and very important, it would create solidarity among the volunteers who together executed their country's highest ideals.[28]

In practice, unfortunately, it has been found that successful action usually requires leadership as well as widespread participation. Even though

[26] Power and the capacity to do violence simply are not congruent. Anyone who has reflected on the capacity of the Vietcong to withstand the U.S. Army is aware of that.
[27] The terms *micro-resistance* and *honeycomb* sound similar to Sharp's *decentralized solidarity*. They are drawn from a description by George Kennan of underground resistance movements. See William Miller, *Nonviolence, A Christian Interpretation* (New York: Schocken Books, 1966), pp. 99–107.
[28] There has also been some discussion about creating an international peace force that would physically interpose itself between warring parties. So far this idea has had little support. Neither a method nor the necessary understanding has been developed for it. It is hard to interpose oneself between ABMs and bombs and villagers; it is also hard to build solidarity among various nationals for a goal so general as world peace.

nonviolent resistance advocates have tried to protect their organizations by not making them dependent on particular leadership, the fact remains that the most successful efforts have had a special kind of leadership.[29] During its heyday, SNCC tried to maintain pure participatory democracy; CORE, on the other hand, worked as a rotating, representative democracy; SCLC's Martin Luther King, Jr., considered himself a "living symbol"; but Gandhi proclaimed himself a "dictator." That is, he acted always on the dictates of his own conscience although he also acknowledged that his power rested on his followers' good will, acceptance, and cooperation.[30] Whatever their formal relationship with their followers, nonviolent leaders must accomplish certain basic tasks: inspiration of the resisters, winning of respect from the opposition, and their own survival.

Collective nonviolent resistance seems to be used most often in the interest of the less privileged or in defense of a homeland. Because its power is essentially that of refusal, or of the veto, it is also advantaged when its stance is defensive. This can mean either that the resisters are opposed to change or that they have seized an initiative, created a change, and are now defending it.

Resistance is also made easier in a complex, interdependent society. The very technology that seems to make a totalitarian government possible also makes it vulnerable. While intelligence services can compile large amounts of data, their secrets can also be leaked to millions of citizens in a single news broadcast. While the government can fly hundreds of paratroopers to the center of a city, a resistance leader can take a jet to another country.

It is also no accident that extremely violent conditions have kindled new interest in nonviolence. It was not by chance that its practice was resurrected by persons concerned about nuclear war and by abused southern blacks. It is a weapon for motivated minorities, for unarmed or relatively defenseless majorities, and for equals who can agree on rules for regulating their relationship even if they can agree on little else. It is a weapon rooted not in weakness but in less obvious kinds of strength. As others have said, it involves *trans*armament, not *dis*armament; that is, it involves not the abandonment of power, but the transformation of dormant power into useful but nondestructive power.

Still, the crucial thing about nonviolent technique, as with all technique, is knowing when and how to use it. It must be used to further clearly defined goals; one must not let himself be used by it and one must not respond inappropriately simply because he has learned and successfully used one particular method. The emphasis must always be on control—on seizing the initiative, on using and changing when appropriate any weapon from the arsenal of nonviolent techniques, and on carefully maintaining the integrity and solidarity of one's group.

What remains to be seen is whether foresight, discussion, planning, and practice can significantly strengthen this collective kind of resistance, which has heretofore been spontaneous, unorganized, and only sometimes sufficient.

---

[29] Because they are not defended with violence, the leaders of nonviolent resistance, and not their followers, are the first, not the last, to be killed or punished. This may be another reason why elite members of society are not enthusiastic about practicing it.
[30] Jawaharlal Nehru, *Toward Freedom* (New York: John Day Co., 1942), p. 53.

# 5    Combined and Contrasting Explanations of Nonviolent Resistance

*The best possible approximations to love are also the most realistic social methods.*
                                    Harvey Seifert, *Conquest by Suffering*

No image is indefinitely sustained; any perception is quickly complemented and supplemented by other views from slightly varied perspectives. Few consistently think of men as single atoms whose society consists of a series of individual encounters, and few systematically reflect on human experience as a struggle between abstract powers in which the individual is, at best, a participant. For this reason some students of nonviolent resistance and most of its practitioners have attempted to forge an explanation of nonviolence that combines both the individual and the collective views of human behavior. Some have even attempted a threefold synthesis. They have added to the secular views the perspective of traditional Christianity. That is, they have tried to explain nonviolence in relation to the individual, to the group, and to God; they have drawn on psychology, sociology, and the Bible.

Because most of those who use nonviolent resistance eclectically try to confront life as it actually is, their approach to it is often through an examination of case studies of real or alleged nonviolent practice or through their own practice of nonviolence. They try to induce generalizations from narratives and activities instead of trying to deduce rules or conclusions from fundamental principles or assumptions. These synthesizers seek primarily to understand, to comprehend, and to act effectively. Their concern is with success more than with coherence or clarity.

## The Christian View of Nonviolent Resistance

There are at least two reasons for examining the conventional Christian attitude toward violence and nonviolence. One is that the nonviolent tradition in this country has long been closely associated with Christianity, and especially with certain Protestant sects. What must be made clear here is that this association is unusual in that mainstream Christianity is not nonviolent. The association between nonviolence and Christianity comes about not because religious people practice nonviolent resistance but because nonviolent resisters tend to be religious. They tend to be so because commitment to nonviolence means willingness to risk death, and this requires a very deep commitment—if not a conventionally religious one, at least one on that order of magnitude. The second reason for examining the traditional Christian position on nonviolence is that this view seems to coincide closely with that of the U.S. public's view. Even if one is not a Christian—or if one is but lacks theological training or understanding—simply by being a part of modern American culture one is likely to take a position quite close to that of traditional Christianity.

Christian theology limits both commitment to nonviolent resistance and belief in the possibility of full understanding. This is because Christianity places great emphasis on man's imperfection and his imperfectability. It causes men not to expect too much; it causes them not to expect too much of nonviolent resistance, or of their own capacity to comprehend. Thus, instead of expecting to find an explanation that will fully elucidate human behavior, the Christian acknowledges that study is much more likely to reveal discrepancies and ambiguities. Instead of expecting nonviolent resistance to end conflict, he hopes only that it will reduce its level. Instead of expecting men to behave justly and peaceably under the direction of nonviolent leadership, he expects that both coercion and violence will have to be used if social order is to be maintained.[1]

Mainstream Christianity is not perfectionist. It aims at being realistic, at dealing with the world as it is rather than as it should be. At the same time it does not simply accept this world; it does hope to improve it. Christian social action tries to be relevant and responsible in its attempts to redeem this world; it tries to act intelligently and with a clear understanding of the limited capacity human beings have for understanding, risk, and sacrifice. Resources and consequences are carefully considered; indeed, their calculation sometimes seems to approach that of Benthamism.[2] Still, mathematics is not everything, for after all has been carefully weighed one fact always remains—for the Christian, God conditions all. It is He who understands all, it is He who dispenses power, it is He who bestows grace, and it is His purpose that is embodied in human history. This means that when something seems to go wrong or is puzzling, the Christian can feel sure there is a reason for it. Even if one does not understand what has happened or is happening, one knows that nothing will defeat God's will. God's good will is assumed.

Christians who advocate nonviolent resistance are often not content to define it negatively; they do not feel its essence lies in abstention or restraint. Instead, they impute to it a meaning close to that of the Greek word *agape*. This is in no way a limited or negative word; it does not mean forbearance, but love. Further, it means more than *eros* (self-fulfilling love) or *philia*

---

[1] It is interesting to note that Gandhi also believed human beings are fallible, but instead of concluding that violence would therefore be required, he interpreted this to mean that one should not use violence on the grounds that one could never be sure if he were justified in inflicting suffering on others.

[2] The philosophy of Jeremy Bentham and the other utilitarians of the eighteenth century, in which decisions are arrived at by weighing pleasure against pain.

(reciprocal love); it refers to that overarching positive love that is manifested in action and that demonstrates "good will" toward all "in God." It both "is God" and "is of God." One gains access to it not by reason or will, but by faith or grace. God is love's "generator"; man is its "transmitter."[3]

Nonviolent resistance and love are not, however, perfectly congruent. Nonviolent resistance can be a loveless technique and love may necessitate the doing of bodily harm. Only under ideal circumstances (which occur never or only transiently) do love and nonviolent resistance fully include each other, and only under those circumstances could a Christian fully commit himself to such resistance.

A Christian's commitment is to agapic love, which may employ physical violence even though it is never violent in spirit, that is, in intent. Similarly mere nonviolence, or nonviolent technique, may be used for unloving purposes and by those who are violent in spirit. Therefore, a Christian frequently must choose between basing his action on nonviolent techniques or on *agape*—on nonviolence or on love. The Christian choice always is love, and this is why the organized church has not strongly endorsed nonviolence. For the most part its support has been circumstantial or proportional—that is, it finds nonviolent resistance appropriate in some situations, or a method that should be used as much as possible.

Just as one's motive or spiritual state is considered relevant to assessing one's behavior, so the spiritual results of one's acts are weighed by the Christian when he assesses nonviolent action. Just as one should act with love even if this entails violence, so one should avoid injury even if it is only spiritual injury. This means that an act that impairs another's self-respect should be avoided; so should an act that causes an individual to betray his friends. Further, an act that damages the spirit may not only not cause any physical injury, it may not even require interaction with another person! One can actually wreak violence on himself; he can afflict his own spirit. To illustrate what he considers spiritual violence, William Miller describes two men. The first chops his neighbor to bits with an axe but afterward suffers great remorse. The second never actually injures anyone, but in his imagination he gleefully devises and inflicts hideous tortures on his friends and neighbors. "Surely," Miller concludes, "the fantasy torturer is a worse specimen of mankind than the actual killer who has repented."[4] Perhaps, but somehow he does not also seem to be the less violent.

The Christian realist expects no terrestrial utopia. While Christians do not feel they must use violence in their relations with one another, they do believe that society as a whole is and will remain "sub-Christian," and therefore that sub-Christian modes of operation will remain generally appropriate to the

---

[3] William Miller, *Nonviolence, A Christian Interpretation* (New York: Schocken Books, 1966), pp. 24–26, 40. This is a good and readily available summary of the traditional Christian position. It also contains a large number of case studies, which are analyzed clearly, concisely, and unsentimentally. Miller, along with Reinhold Niebuhr, is an example of what I refer to as a Christian realist.

[4] Ibid., pp. 33–35.

individual's dealings with the world. Christians further believe that even if they were voluntarily to render themselves vulnerable through unilateral disarmament, they have no right to choose the risk of "the way of the Cross," or redemptive suffering, for others. Thus, even those Christians who advocate and practice nonviolence themselves will often not try to establish it as a policy for others. Some (Dorothy Day, for instance) will not even advise it for others. Interestingly enough, the converse, that others should not make decisions concerning violence binding on Christian advocates of nonviolence, is not usually held to be true. Apparently even nonviolent resisters see their position as deviant rather than normal! Thus, most Christians not only permit but also participate in coercive, forceful, and even violent behavior if it is said to promote the community's good and God's will.

## Proportional Nonviolent Resistance

### Tactical Nonviolent Resistance

William Miller has made a major contribution to the theory of nonviolence by designing a vertical classification for kinds of nonviolent action. It is significant because it deftly and originally deals with the difference between the expedient nonviolent resistance of the Christian realist and the various forms of committed nonviolent resistance. Instead of becoming enmeshed in the question of whether or not one can be somewhat nonviolent, defining particular situations in which one will or will not practice nonviolence (purists say that one either is or is not nonviolent), Miller speaks of three levels of nonviolence usage. He calls them the *subtactical* or *spontaneous,* the *tactical,* and the *strategic.*[5]

By the very offering of this classification, Miller reveals his own view, which is that it is quite possible to have a partial, circumstantial, or existential commitment to nonviolence. At the same time, he accounts for the differences between two quite different kinds of nonviolence by focusing on their scope of commitment. The first kind closely corresponds to the position taken by many advocates of individual nonviolence and is referred to as a subtactical, or spontaneous, commitment; the third, or strategic, kind of nonviolence comes close to the view held by the proponents of collective nonviolence; Miller and most Christians seem to fit in the remaining category, which is the one endorsing tactical nonviolence.

The subtactical use of nonviolence usually involves little long-range planning and only a limited number of people. It can be a spontaneous expression of their good will or utter despair, or it can involve a carefully conceived and executed act of witness that seeks either to maintain the actor's integrity or to dramatize his social concern. Often the deed done does not seem related to a complete analysis of the problem at hand or of the ways in which it might be solved. Nonviolence seems almost to be an end in itself for the subtactical group.

---

[5] Ibid., pp. 61–70.

In contrast, both the tactical and strategic views of nonviolent resistance perceive it as a means. The tactical view is the more flexible; it utilizes nonviolent resistance only when it can be expected to succeed, and it uses other means either in conjunction with or sequentially to it. The focus is on the end, and the sufficiency of the means. This coincides both with the traditional Christian position and with the usual secular position.

To think of nonviolent resistance as a strategy is to think of it on the grandest scale of all. It is to believe that nonviolent resistance is the one and the only way to maximize success. Thus, the strategic thinker can be as absolutely committed to nonviolence as is the person who uses nonviolent resistance subtactically. However, the implication of calling it a strategy is that one believes it will be the most economic and effective way of achieving a particular goal, not just the most moral way. What is required is great wisdom and foresight, much planning and skillful organization.

How does it happen that the Christian, a person with a profound moral commitment, usually adopts a tactical point of view? It comes from his morality, from his commitment to participating in the affairs of this world as best he is able. How far he feels able is linked to his perception of this world as imperfect and not fully knowable. Thus, while he believes he must do his best, he believes that that is all he can do. It means that even if he meets every situation with love and hope for redemption, because of man's proud and competitive nature the most he as a Christian can hope to achieve is a normalization or regularization of relationships. The guideline for action is not purity, but proportion. No limit is placed on means except that they should be tailored to fit both the goal pursued and the obstacles to be overcome.

## The Just War and Civil Disobedience

While there is no defined Christian doctrine concerning nonviolent resistance, there is a conventional position on war. It is that there are "just" and "unjust" wars and that both are a part of the human condition. The criteria for recognizing a just war are: (1) that it be undertaken with good intentions; (2) that it be proclaimed by a legitimate authority; (3) that it be expected to succeed; (4) that the means used be in proportion to the ends that will be won; and (5) that it be a last resort. Generally, to justify war is to justify violence and these justifications for war seem to be a good guide to the conditions under which one might expect the Christian to go beyond nonviolent resistance.

First, one must be properly motivated (well-intentioned). Second, the means must be necessary (a last resort), sufficient (successful), and appropriate (the gain must outweigh the loss). Finally, the action must be legitimate (sanctioned by appropriate authority). This last point significantly undercuts any regular use of nonviolent resistance by Christians. Illegal action is virtually barred for them; and while nonviolent resistance does not necessarily involve illegal action, the two cannot always be easily dissociated.

Most people believe that force, or legal violence, and law, the threat of force, are essential to the maintenance of order; they believe also that order is essential to purposive human action. Apart from the fact that law is supposed to embody justice, law and its concomitant, force, have been justified in several ways. One is that law is said to represent the collective will. A second is that it impersonally effects policy decisions: it is not enforced by those who will directly benefit. A third is that it creates a regular or predictable environment. Whatever the justification, respect for legal or legitimate authority is great. It is so great that there is even a tendency to sanction illegal or extralegal acts if they are done by "officials." Sometimes this sanction is explained as being a part of "executive" authority; sometimes it is just explained as "necessary."

While there is high tolerance for illegal or extralegal violence done by government officials, there is virtually no tolerance for that done by private citizens. Thus, Christians and most Americans face a very real crisis of conscience when they first contemplate illegal nonviolent action (civil disobedience).

Thoreau's argument that one's highest obligation is to his conscience has not won wide support because that view supposes men to possess a uniformly accurate sense of what is moral. Whether true or not, this belief has not yet been able to sustain either a large or a long-lived community. Men simply prefer continuity, order, and predictability over perfect respect for conscience. Thus, it is generally thought that at a very minimum an individual who exercises his right to disobey should submit willingly to charges pressed or penalties enacted. By doing so, he can display his respect for authority and for the principle of law at the same time that he expresses concern over a particular law or official action.

The Christian is also charged to consider factors other than public order and his conscience before deciding whether or not to do an illegal act. Most of these other considerations reduce the likelihood that he will disobey. They include determining whether or not the expression of his conscience would chiefly be egoistic and self-indulgent, and examining what effect his disobedient action would have on the consciences of others who might be either overridden or thwarted by his action. He might also be asked to consider whether civil disobedience is being used to raise a test case, that is, to establish legal boundaries, or if it is a bid for publicity, or a way to short-circuit the governmental process in the interest of a self-selected oligarchy. Important as these items may be, for most persons the crucial reservation remains the effect deliberate illegal behavior has on the stability of government. Stability is highly valued in Christian political thought, and by most Americans as well. Few wish to undermine general respect for law and for order; when law and order do not coincide, most would argue that order is the more important.

## Revolution and Nonviolent Resistance

All the above points question whether or not a wrong is serious enough to merit the use of nonviolent resistance. The obverse and crucial question concerning nonviolent resistance and proportion is whether it is powerful enough to meet any challenge presented or change required. For instance, can nonviolent resistance produce radical and/or revolutionary change? Let us assume that radical change is fundamental change, that it involves more than alterations of a formal nature and more than a change in personnel or rotation of elites. Often radical change is automatically thought of as the product of violence; however, there is some reason to argue that radical change can *only* be achieved nonviolently, or at least, that it can only occur when it could have occurred nonviolently.

The relevant argument is that no fundamental change occurs when one group of officials is simply replaced by a stronger group of officials, even if they do call themselves radicals. As long as the form and the apparatus of the state remain unchanged, radicals inevitably become corrupt. They inevitably come to command the same old machinery in the same old way even though different persons or groups are benefited.[6] For real change to occur, the old order must wither rather than be wrested away; its power must erode or dissolve. This process is not only nonviolent, it often goes more or less unnoted. Its essence is not assassination or seizure of command posts; it is ordinary disorganization and disobedience. It is citizens disbelieving their officials, industrialists neglecting to pay their taxes, demonstrators refusing to disperse, onlookers refusing to interfere, and finally, soldiers failing to fire. Frequently this kind of disintegrating situation comes in the wake of an unsuccessful war: a government drains its society without producing a reward; its citizens begin to withhold their resources; the government becomes progressively less effective and respect and regard for it decrease; finally, citizen resistance brings it to an end.

A revolution does not end with the destruction of the old order; a new order must be established, and it is here that nonviolent resistance may falter because group nonviolent resistance, at least, is limited to approving or disapproving. It has the power to endorse or to veto. It can dispose, but someone or some group must propose. The crucial question is not whether nonviolent resistance can subdue substantial power, but whether it can devise and propose new rules and new structures.

The revolutionary sequence outlined by Crane Brinton in his *Anatomy of a Revolution* has become a classic.[7] His analysis is based on a comparison of the English, American, French, and Russian revolutions. In it certain conditions are described as symptomatic of the coming of revolution. They include improving conditions (increasing and differently distributing power of various kinds); desertion of the regime by the intellectuals (decreased approval of the government, decreased acceptance of authority); and inefficient government (decreased citizen

---

[6] Corruption of resisters and revolutionaries, can occur in at least one of three ways. They can be co-opted or induced to join the organization they oppose by offers of opportunities to advance their purposes; they can abandon idealistic goals for hedonistic goals; or they can adhere to their purposes while acting like or using the methods of their opponents (for example, by expanding surveillance, by requiring oaths of loyalty, or by ordering the arbitrary treatment of groups of citizens).

[7] Crane Brinton, *Anatomy of a Revolution* (New York: W. W. Norton and Co., 1938). For other analyses of revolution, see D. J. Goodspeed, *The Conspirators: A Study of the Coup d'Etat* (New York: Viking Press, 1962); Edward Luttwak, *Coup d'Etat* (New York: Alfred A. Knopf, 1969); and Michael Walzer, *Revolution of the Saints* (New York: Atheneum Publishers, 1968).

cooperation). Brinton's analysis also outlines three stages through which a revolutionary government usually passes. They are (1) moderate, broadly based government, (2) a drive toward extremism under a "reign of terror and virtue," and (3) the advent of a strong man.

It is not at all clear that nonviolent resistance can effectively control the forces unleashed in this sequence; yet it does seem fair to expect a radical leader, whether violent or nonviolent, to see his followers through the full cycle. A leader who abandons his followers once revolution has begun or a leader who is unprepared for the time when extremists or strong men come on the scene must be considered irresponsible. Still, Brinton's scheme may not be universally applicable. In particular, it may be that a nonviolent revolution would not follow the same pattern. For instance, the nonviolent revolutions of India and Ghana did not produce the same sequence of postrevolutionary developments, although each was dependent on strong leadership. Even the American Revolution does not fit Brinton's paradigm very well. On the other hand, it may be that what the Indian, Ghanaian, and American revolutions had in common was not method but purpose—independence from England. In each case, the principal goal was to shuck off a foreign minority and its superstructure; alteration of the basic social structure of these societies did not occur. For this reason, some might even say that revolutions did not occur.

Even if one does grant that India and Ghana experienced a revolution, one must inquire carefully as to whether or not nonviolent resistance was really responsible for the victories. The fact is that in both cases Britain left more or less voluntarily after suffering severe losses in World War II. Even the U.S. revolution owed much of its success to England's other enemies. Probably there have not yet been any consciously planned or executed absolutely nonviolent revolutions. The question is, Will there be, or are the changes in potential for power that make radical nonviolent change possible so subtle that those involved cannot identify them? That is, can capacity for change only be viewed historically or from a distance, or can resisters analyze their own position, advocate their own cause, and take action into their own hands?[8]

## Combined Explanations of Nonviolent Resistance

Many Americans, Christian and non-Christian, believe that nonviolent resistance should not be considered a sufficient means of action, but that it should be thought of as a tool to be used in combination with many others and as a part of a larger strategy either of legal change or perhaps of violent revolution. An excellent example of how nonviolent resistance can be tactically and conjointly used is found in the Montgomery, Alabama, bus boycott led by Martin Luther King, Jr. In that case a long-term, legal, nonviolent campaign requiring intricate planning and consuming quantities of time and energy was used in tandem with

---

[8] It has been suggested that participants in mass movements do not understand the nature of their action. See Carl J. Friedrich, ed., *Nomos VIII Revolution* (New York: Atherton Press, 1966), p. 17.

a series of legal challenges to win desegregation of the city buses; nonviolent resistance was *not* the single means chosen to achieve the goal. Indeed, victory came with a United States Supreme Court decision just as the whole resistance campaign seemed on the verge of collapsing. Still, it may be that the long-term, nonviolent resistance practiced by the black community made city and bus officials more willing to comply with the Court's decision than they would have been if the struggle had been conducted exclusively through the judicial process. It may also be that the Supreme Court would never have addressed the question at all if it had not been for the dramatic and disciplined campaign.

Just as tacticians of nonviolent resistance do not use it in isolation, most of them do not think of it entirely within either a psychological or a sociological framework. Therefore, campaign plans are alternately based on concepts of "the nature of man," and on analysis of society's "lines of repercussion," that is, of what parts of society will react to what stimuli.

The tactician, who is only situationally committed to nonviolence, probably prepares himself and his followers for action somewhat differently from persons whose commitment is total. His chief emphasis is on learning and adhering to a code of conduct. That is, he emphasizes reproduction of the behavior of the nonviolent resister, not his belief. What is sought is a disciplined response that will not vary under stress. Commitment is not required; the leader is not even committed! Recruits for tactical nonviolence are frequently asked, in addition to memorizing a code of discipline, to rehearse the techniques of nonviolence until they become habitual. The goal is to eliminate uncertainty and the possibility of being surprised. These exercises are also thought to increase the resister's understanding of himself and his opponent. In short, participation in this kind of sociodrama is supposed to yield a closer appreciation of the world as it really is.[9] But not only are individuals prepared as individuals, groups are also prepared as groups. Slogans and symbols that are clear, simple, and rhythmic are shared among the resisters. Shared songs and stories are also used to enhance a feeling of community. Still, the most important element of all is probably shared experience. SNCC volunteers found that Northern "Friends of SNCC" simply could not involve themselves in the same way as those who had "gone South"; they could not even sing "We Shall Overcome" properly. To some degree, participating in constructive programs creates a feeling of community, but the most binding experience probably belongs to those who have risked their lives together.

The tactical resister must also be an excellent calculator. He must analyze society's organization and must understand the dynamics of change. He must recognize that nonviolent activity can be a publicity-seeking device, or a way of disciplining or purifying oneself as well as a way of bringing about change. He must recognize that it can produce negative as well as positive effects, that it can bring scorn and contempt on one, and that because voluntary suffering

---

[9] Theodore Olson and Gordon Christiansen, *The Grindstone Experiment* (Toronto: Canadian Friends Service Committee, 1966) provides an interesting account of a 36-hour sociodrama in which tension became so high the experiment had to be stopped before it had run its course.

is real suffering, it is something to avoid, not to promote. He must know, too, that as conflict increases, repression will increase. He must then decide whether repression will finally succeed in smothering resistance or whether it will lead to revulsion, for it is true that change often comes when things look most bleak. This is because at the same time that punishment is increasing, more and more groups may be becoming involved and their views of the represser's actions may be moving from approval, to toleration, to disgust, to intervention.

The tactician must also decide whether to present a conciliatory image of constantly trying to establish rapport with his foe or a strong image of standing on absolute moral principle. He must weigh the consequences of group activity, realizing that it can have either a positive or a negative effect. For instance, strength can be demonstrated and morale improved when action is taken with a large number of others. On the other hand, discipline and control decrease with increased size. The tactician must therefore strike a proper balance between decentralization and efficiency. In sum, the tactician must combine nonviolent resistance with other methods of social change and control, and also combine the psychological and sociological views of nonviolence. Sometimes he will focus on social structure and organization and sometimes on the interaction of individuals. Although this alternation of approaches lacks intellectual elegance, one is comforted by remembering that a more rigorous analysis (whether theological, sociological or psychological) would also be more limited and further from life as it is experienced by the resister, his opponents, his critics, the author, and the reader of this book.

The combined approach is the most regular approach. It is usual to alternate between attacking those who hurt and assisting those who are hurt, between invoking the authority of Gandhi and that of the guerrilla, between expressing respect for others and demanding it for oneself. The opening editorial of *Liberation*'s first issue sums up this theme well: "The politics of the future requires a creative synthesis of the individual ethical insights of the great religious leaders and the collective social concern of the great revolutionists."[10]

A number of individuals beside William Miller developed an eclectic approach to nonviolence. They include Harvey Seifert, A. J. Muste, and Martin Luther King, Jr. Seifert is a theorist; Muste and King were both primarily activists, the former in the labor and peace movements, the latter in the civil rights movement.

Harvey Seifert summarizes nonviolence in the words of the title of a book he published in 1965, *Conquest by Suffering.* In this volume, one of the most enlightening on the subject, he assesses "the process and prospects of nonviolent resistance." His view is encompassing. He argues that the purpose of nonviolent resistance can be either to serve as a "witness" to an ethical code or religious belief or to act as a force to promote social change. He argues, too, that it can be practiced individually or collectively, and that it can use a wide

---

[10] Editorial Statement, Issue No. 1, *Liberation,* March 1956, p. 5. See also Arthur Waskow, "Gandhi and Guerrilla," *Liberation,* November 1967, pp. 26–28; and Barbara Deming, "On Revolution and Equilibrium," *Liberation,* February 1968, pp. 10–21.

variety of techniques, including noncooperation, civil disobedience, and self-suffering.

In describing the resistance process, Seifert refers to it as a trial not of power but of one group's persistence versus another's severity. Seifert also makes several interesting arguments concerning the relationship between morality and efficacy. First, he notes that a moral position increases one's chance of being effective because the sincerity and intensity of one's convictions give one the strength to persist in a struggle. Second, he warns that he who believes he acts morally is likely to justify any means on the grounds that they contribute to a greater good. Third, he argues that action taken for moral reasons is not justified unless it can be expected to succeed. He does not believe in futility; he does not urge nonviolent resistance if social conditions seem to guarantee serious losses or defeat.

Seifert shows no compunction at all about using coercion to accomplish desired ends. His concern basically is with achieving a measured response —one that accomplishes one's goal with a minimal use of coercion, but that does not necessarily rule out any particular means, even violent ones. The reasoning that leads him to this conclusion is, first, that man is fallible and imperfectible; and second, that nonviolent resistance never exists in isolation: it always serves as an "adjunct" to the more usual methods of change, such as education, the political process, and war.

Seifert addresses the same problems as Miller and other Christian realists at the same moment in time and reaches similar conclusions: (1) It is the "mix" of reason and emotion and of persuasion and coercion that makes nonviolent resistance, (2) nonviolence is more effective than most people believe, but less effective than its strongest adherents claim.

A. J. Muste and Martin Luther King, Jr., were two American activists who sought to practice "combined" versions of nonviolence. Muste began his career as a Congregational clergyman. His pacifist stand in World War I brought criticism from his congregation, however, and he resigned from his pastorate. During and after the war he devoted himself to work with the American Civil Liberties Union, the Fellowship of Reconciliation, the American Friends, and the labor movement. In a strike in Lawrence, Massachusetts, in 1919 he was beaten and jailed. For the rest of the 1920s and during the 1930s his chief cause was that of labor. When things were bleakest, from 1933 to 1936, he even became a Trotskyite; soon afterwards, however, he reconverted to being what he called a Calvinist-Socialist. During World War II, Muste worked to abolish the draft, and after 1948 he became an advocate of unilateral disarmament.

Muste, like Richard Gregg, referred to nonviolence as moral jiu-jitsu, and believed that spiritual force was as real as physical force. He himself lived by an individual code of behavior consisting of telling the truth, admitting error, and refusing to fear. At the same time, Muste, like the collectivists, was committed to the building of a "mass, direct action [peace] movement," to "confounding and overcoming an enemy," and to "deal[ing] with others on the basis of reality." Muste clearly tried to unite Christianity, psychology, and sociology. He expected the moral and the effective to coincide; he assumed that theory and practice would easily merge, but it is not quite so clear that he accepted the use of both coercive and noncoercive techniques. Muste's language is combative, but his explanation of nonviolent resistance as having its effect by undermining the enemy's morale and by removing his will to conquer, as well as his conclusion that the pacifist's purpose is to change people not to defeat them, seems to set him somewhat apart from other Christian realists.[11]

The Reverend Martin Luther King, Jr., was probably the nonviolent activist who most fully practiced a combined form of resistance. King clearly recognized the combined nature of his thought and action, as is shown in his essay "A Pilgrimage to Nonviolence." There he specifically refers to nonviolent resistance as being like the synthesis in Hegelian philosophy because it seeks to reconcile the truths of two opposites—"acquiescence and violence"—while avoiding "the extremes and immoralities of both." King speaks also of the need to alternate rhythmically between "attacking the causes and healing the effects," and of the need to use both "a tough mind and a tender heart."

King also assumed the merging of moral and effective measures in nonviolence. A few quotations will illustrate this: "Violence is impractical and immoral." "Nonviolence . . . is a powerful and just weapon." "Both a practical and moral answer to the Negro's cry for justice, nonviolent direct action proved that it could win victories."[12]

King did have a personal commitment to nonviolent resistance; he was not prepared to use violence in certain situations as many other Christian thinkers are, but he did not hesitate to use a mixture of noncoercive and coercive means so long as physical violence was not involved. His rhetoric, with its almost violent appeal to nonviolence, reflects this. In his introduction to Robert Williams's book *Negroes with Guns* (one of the first books to vigorously argue that American blacks should arm themselves for self-defense), King proclaimed, "We will never let them rest"; "We will fight with the weapon of love." Elsewhere, he asserted that he and his followers would "never allow the conscience of the oppressor to slumber." He warned his foe, "We shall wear you down by our capacity to suffer"; and in one instance he admonished his supporters to "love the hell out of those white people."[13]

King's rhetoric also contains numerous religious references. He sought to free his oppressor from his sins. He believed unearned suffering was redemptive, and that prayer is an important aid to decision-making.

At bottom, however, King's thought and action were founded on his

---

[11] Muste's autobiography has been published in installments in the journal *Liberation*. Nat Hentoff has also published a biography of Muste, entitled *Peace Agitator*, most of which appeared first in the *New Yorker*.

[12] Martin Luther King, Jr., *Stride Toward Freedom* (New York: Harper, 1958), pp. 213, 224; and *Strength to Love* (New York: Harper, 1963), pp. 1, 38. For other examples see King, *Stride Toward Freedom*, pp. 87, 213; and *Why We Can't Wait* (New York: Harper & Row, 1964), p. 14.

[13] King, *Stride Toward Freedom*, p. 212; *Strength to Love*, p. 49; and Stephen Rose, "Test for Nonviolence," *Christian Century*, May 29, 1963, p. 714.

personal faith that the universe is under the control of a loving purpose that is on the side of justice, and that man's purpose in life is to accomplish a twofold integration: the first vertical, with God, and the second horizontal, with men.[14] Thus, he argued, resistance and nonviolence do not depend exclusively on the efforts of either man or God, but on "both man and God, made one in a marvelous unity of purpose through an overflowing love as the free gift of himself on the part of God and by perfect obedience and receptivity on the part of man [which] can transform the old into the new and drive out the deadly cancer of sin." King did not believe, however, that resistance and nonviolence are intrinsically good. He recognized that the tactics of nonviolence could become a new kind of spiritual violence, for to him the crucial element in struggle was not resistance but love or reconciliation, and the ultimate end was not victory but "the creation of the beloved community."[15]

## Contrasting Explanations of Nonviolent Resistance

It is easy to understand why combined explanations are appealing. They incorporate the most attractive aspects of a number of theories. They are as inclusive as possible of available knowledge, they assume both morality and efficacy, they include a wide variety of actions, and they link theory to practice. Unfortunately, even though the theories of group and individual nonviolent resistance are used together, intellectually they do not really work together. For the most part, their combination amounts to sheer assertion rather than valid interrelation. Any apparent unity of nonviolent thought seems to depend more on veiled confusion than on a clear perception of complementarity.

Does this mean that there is no relationship between the varying explanations? Does it mean that the explanations are neither reconcilable nor sequential? Or is there a cogent way of describing what seems to be a symbiosis, a close association of dissimilars based on advantages for both? Since the elision of different views seems to create greater resources for struggle and to provide greater or alternative forms of satisfaction once struggle is done, one must expect a combination of the explanations to occur. The question is how. How are the different elements to be fitted together? In an attempt to construct a comprehensive explanation, let us begin by once again contrasting the two basic views of nonviolent resistance.

The essence of nonviolent resistance is nonroutine self-restraint. Its activities range from solitary fasts to large-scale boycotts. Its practitioners include infinitely patient Friends and stridently impatient members of ad hoc protest groups. This variety seems principally to proceed from how one sees the world, and this depends, at least in part, on where one stands. One particular phenomenon is called trees by some and a forest by others. Time for some means the

---

14 King, *Why We Can't Wait*, p. 28; and Lerone Bennett, Jr., *What Manner of Man* (Chicago: Johnson Publishing Co., 1964), pp. 159, 186. See also King, *Strength to Love*, p. 172; *Stride Toward Freedom*, pp. 36, 106.
15 King, *Strength to Love*, p. 152; Bennett, *What Manner of Man*, p. 114.

present, for others, a decade into the past or future, and for still others, centuries, periods, or eras.

To view something first with the naked eye and then with a microscope or a telescope is usually to amplify one's perspective and to increase understanding. The tragedy of present-day thought on nonviolent resistance is that differences in the scale of the discussion have too often produced contradiction and confusion rather than comprehension. In fact, they have produced two almost polar sets of beliefs.[16]

One set sees the world as composed of individual human beings, each of whom has a common and high purpose for his existence and each of whom can have a powerful social effect through his individual action. Truth, morality, and capacity are seen as congruent. Philosophy and potency, then, are one: to speak truth is to exercise power. Plato's philosopher-king represents well the ideal individual nonviolent resister. Because goodness and wisdom are thought to yield effectiveness, cultivation of oneself becomes an important and legitimate social act.

The second perspective focuses on organized society. It perceives groups and forces and particular purposes. It does not deny the importance of individual initiative or the morality of nonviolent resistance; it simply concerns itself with other affairs. It focuses on the changing, not on the unchanging. It concentrates on power, not on truth. In the most literal sense, it aims at realizing a constantly consented-to society, in which the people genuinely are sovereign.

The individual resister's interest in an understanding of nonviolent resistance and his need for this understanding proceed from his devotion to truth and morality. He is committed to an ethical imperative that prohibits the doing of injury. His belief primarily affects himself; it prescribes the way he should (or, primarily, should not) behave. It does not dictate a goal he should seek nor does it focus on other people except perhaps to seek to be an example for them.

The noninjury imperative can usually be deduced from certain assumptions concerning the unity of the universe, its apparent disunity, and the need to dispel the illusion of disunity and to realize unity. The action imperative is that conscience, which all men have in common, must be cherished. It must not only be cherished, it must be obeyed. One must attune oneself to his own conscience and obey it, and he must encourage others to obey theirs. He must never tempt or coerce others to violate their principles, although, if necessary, he must assist them to become conscious of their consciences and responsive to them.

To accomplish this, the individual nonviolent resister may use reason, emotion, or both. He may use language precisely or artistically or he may abandon

---

[16] The problem of scale is accentuated when one's subject is international relations. Then international considerations must be added to sociological and psychological considerations. Two especially competent attempts to relate varying perspectives are Kenneth Waltz, *Man, The State and War* (New York: Columbia University Press, 1959), and John P. Lovell, *Foreign Policy in Perspective: Strategy—Adaptation—Decision Making* (New York: Holt, Rinehart and Winston, 1970).

it for some kind of nonverbal or empathic communication. An especially favored method of communication is the display of voluntary, unmerited, and unnecessary suffering.

Because this approach to nonviolent resistance presumes that all humans can be made receptive to conscience and that all consciences share "truth," it is generally concluded that nonviolent resistance is appropriate to all times and to all circumstances. In theory, one's status or the numbers of those resisting should have no bearing on its efficacy. Because this kind of resistance works by creating a new awareness in one's foe, by changing his attitude or his perception of what is, it is said to work through conversion or persuasion. Coercion, which works by changing an adversary's options (by using the technique either of the carrot or of the stick), is considered a violation of his conscience and to result in decreased rather than increased communication. It is therefore tabooed by the disciples of individual nonviolent resistance.

Advocates of this kind of resistance rate high marks for their integrity and aspirations, but to many their view seems flawed. First, its simple denial of the reality of conflict seems to fly in the face of human experience. Second, this approach stresses intuition and empathy and the mobilization of behavior resulting from such psychological states as guilt, love, and surprise, but little attempt is made systematically to examine these nonrational states. This is not to say that professional literature on these subjects goes uncited; it is to say that no allegiance is given any particular school of psychology from which an explanation is systematically deduced or with which compatibility is established. What seems to happen is that a variety of sources are drawn on for the purpose of persuasion rather than for the purpose of underpinning and supporting a theory evidentially. Third, although there is discussion of the importance of organization and of the application of group nonviolence, this theory's basic perception remains that of the individual as a social isolate with a moral mission to fulfill, or else that of an individual who is social but who is bound to all human beings by equally strong ties. While either of these assumptions is theoretically tidy, both poorly reflect the varieties of human relationships men actually experience. Fourth, the theory is apocalyptic in its time orientation. Nonviolence is said to be efficacious, but no time is set within which some change must occur in order to validate this assertion. Advocates simultaneously put off making a judgment to the indefinite future (or occasionally to another world) and apocalyptically proclaim that change can occur at any time and be both total and instantaneous. Finally, because action is too often urged on by slogans such as "a good tree bears good fruit" or because it is too often based on what can only be called a self-fulfilling prophecy (treat your opponent as though you expect him to behave well and he will behave well), the mood of this kind of nonviolent theory is sometimes perfectionistic, chiliastic, and anarchistic. This, of course, is one of the basic criticisms of individual nonviolent resistance made by advocates of group nonviolent resistance and by Christian realists. Both groups take great pains to avoid projecting such a mood.

In contrast, exponents of group nonviolence do not assume that the perceived world is unreal, and the unseen real. They do not attempt to substitute the power of truth for that of coercion. Their goal is to wage an effective, goal-oriented struggle against an apparently stronger opponent.

Those holding this general view accept conflict as inevitable and perhaps even as desirable. They view nonviolent resistance not as a way to end conflict, but as an economical way to conduct it. Joan Bondurant has discussed this kind of nonviolent resistance as "symbolic violence"; she has also compared it to guerrilla warfare. From her discussion it might be concluded that a guerrilla or "limited" war fought by two major powers through the medium of a third country's civil war is a way of ritualizing the major parties' struggle and thus represents a constructive step toward nonviolence.[17] The so-called cold war of the 1950s might be considered another example of this ritualization process, while the 1960s space race may be regarded as an even more successful way of debrutalizing conflict.

By entrusting the determination of policy to the winner of what is essentially a trial-by-ordeal, group nonviolent resistance theory puts itself in accord with the principles of laissez-faire economics, academic freedom, and free speech. Each of these concepts assumes that congruency between "right" and "might" can best be achieved by determining each by a like process—that process being competition, or struggle. It is the lack of congruence between these two abstractions, right and might, that gives birth both to political conflict and to political theory.

According to the theory of group nonviolent resistance, the rules governing the conduct of nonviolent trial *do* preclude the use or threat of violence. They do not, however, forbid the use of coercion. Nor is it at all clear that the results of legal violence or of violence done by a third party on one's behalf must be renounced or denounced. Quakers do take advantage of the judicial process, and are happy to have the law enforced. Civil rights leaders frequently call for judicial or federal intervention on their behalf, and some have not been loath to warn of the possibility of violence by their supporters if their pleas go unheeded. The reasoning that supports such a position may be not that violence should be absolutely prohibited, but that it should never be used to further one's own interest because self-interest blinds one as to how he is using power. Further, if one's cause is truly just, others will act as one's protector.

While individual nonviolent resistance leads to an anarchistic political philosophy, group nonviolent resistance is usually said to be democratic. Although the argument has not been formally and definitively made, it apparently hinges on defining democracy not by its social product or the quality of its civil life, but by the participation in decision making it offers, and by the power it assigns the

---

[17] Bondurant does *not* approve either of guerrilla warfare or of symbolic violence. Her interpretation of nonviolence is dialectical and Gandhian; it is complex, but well worth investigating. See Joan Bondurant, *Conquest of Violence* (Berkeley: University of California Press, 1965); "Paraguerrilla Strategy," *Journal of Conflict Resolution* 7, 3 (September 1963): 235–45; and "Satyagraha versus Duragraha: The Limits of Symbolic Violence," in *Gandhi: His Relevance for Our Times,* ed. G. Ramachandran and T. K. Mahadevan (Bombay: Bharatiya Vidya Bhavan, 1964).

majority. The argument is that nonviolent resistance can be successful only if it wins at least the passive support of most of society's members; therefore, when nonviolent resistance is successful, it is automatically "democratic" even if it wins by going outside the boundaries of law, and even if this is done in a country that considers itself democratic. Again, nonviolence is said to be democratic by definition if it succeeds.

Acceptance of this apparently paradoxical argument is made easy if one agrees, first, that any system of representation or any established institution necessarily distorts communication, and second, that nonviolent resistance, which provides for personal participation by all or any members of a society, is by definition the most direct, and therefore the most democratic mode of expressing policy preferences.

A second argument for the inherent democracy of nonviolent resistance slightly modifies the preceding exposition by assuming that the quality of votes cast should be considered as well as their quantity. If the quality of a vote is measured by the intensity of the conviction by which it is supported rather than by its logic or by its morality, proponents of group nonviolent resistance can effectively argue that such an aspect of the democratic ideal is elegantly incorporated in their type of resistance. This is because intensity of conviction can be vividly demonstrated by the resister's persistence and by his willingness to suffer or risk suffering.

Because group nonviolent resistance has the choice of trying to attain its ends either through persuasion (increasing communication or improving perception) or through coercion (changing options, either by inducement—offering increased cooperation—or by sanction—practicing a decrease in cooperation), it almost necessarily leads to a more calculating style of decision making than that practiced by adherents of individual nonviolent resistance. The variables to be manipulated or the considerations to be made are further increased by the fact that the working unit is the group instead of the individual. This means that attention must be given to recruiting and training both leaders and members; lines of responsibility and modes of decision making must be established and ways to maintain morale must be devised. Because of the amount of analysis and planning required by any large-scale and/or long-term group project, this form of nonviolent resistance is sometime regarded as being overly manipulative and as requiring hierarchy, that is, first-class and second-class resisters. This explains why one group, SNCC, spent so much of its energy combating internal manipulation and the ever feared possibility of the growth of a structure.

Still, the chief difficulty with this version of nonviolence is that it bases its claim to support on its effectiveness, even though it is almost impossible to prove such a claim. Proof could take one of two forms: (1) empirical data based on case studies; and (2) a logically consistent theory based on assumptions that are widely accepted as valid. As yet, accumulated empirical data from case histories is sparse; therefore, the group approach tends to try to persuade by means of theoretical explanation and deduction rather than through evidence.

This brief recapitulation of explanations of individual and group nonviolent resistance should serve to show why there is such obvious contradiction and confusion about nonviolence when it is taken as a single and whole theory. The two approaches make different assumptions about conflict and draw different conclusions about coercion. The first holds conflict to be unreal and coercion illegitimate. The second expects conflict to be continuous, does not require conversion of the opponent (simple compliance being thought quite satisfactory), and considers coercion a totally appropriate weapon.

A second difference between the two views lies in their ethical orientation. The first emphasizes individual obligation—the duty one has consistently and perfectly to fulfill moral requirements. The second is rooted in an ethic of responsibility that does not permit one to achieve moral excellence by following rules or fulfilling commands. Instead, one is held accountable for making judgment about the probable consequences as opposed to merely the intentions of one's actions; about deeds undone as well as those done; and the acts of others that one might control or influence. The first kind of nonviolent resister engages in strenuous introspection; the second is charged with scrutinizing and criticizing all of society.

Third, although both explanations are predicated on man's essential equality (at least of value), the optimistic assumptions of the first lead inexorably to the conclusion that the optimal form of government is no form—anarchism. The second with its acceptance of conflict, struggle, and power as inherent to life opts for some form of democracy.

A fourth difference lies in the fact that individual nonviolent resistance requires that action be taken by single individuals, by individuals acting in parallel, or possibly by a group executing a unanimous decision. In contrast, group nonviolence is the work of persons acting in concert and its practitioners must address themselves to all the problems raised by the sociologist as well as those posed by the psychologist. Group nonviolent adherents must consider such semipolitical questions as the terms of membership in an organization committed to nonviolence. They must also decide whether the need for solidarity justifies compelling membership. If they decide it does, they must determine which compulsory means are appropriate. Similarly, they must decide whether members can be expelled and, if so, on what grounds. They must be prepared to answer the contention that a nonviolent organization should be as committed to the rehabilitation of spies, provocateurs, and pathologic cases within its own ranks as it is to the changing of outsiders labelled "foe."

Finally, although neither approach specifically makes this distinction, one is forced to conclude that the first theory is rooted in an optimistic belief in man's potential for good, while the linchpin of the second is a pessimistic belief in his potential for destruction.

# 6    Social Change and Nonviolent Power

### Philosopher-Kings and the Sovereign People

Let us see if these contrasting theories can be tied together. The fundamental problem of twentieth-century political thought is not the role of the individual, a concern of eighteenth-century philosophers, nor is it the question of society, an issue belonging to the nineteenth century. It is the relationship between what has been called the elite and the mass. It concerns the few who are individually efficacious, whether their power is public or private, and the many who permit (or do not permit) the elite to act but who themselves are efficacious only as members of a group.

The elite direct the ongoing activities of society. They also define social problems, propose solutions, and mobilize resources for desired change. In doing these activities, the elite must consider the mass. Sometimes they wonder, "What do they want?" Sometimes they only worry, "What will they stand for?" The elite individually and as a group fill the role of the philosopher-king. They are experts; they define the good; they make things seem so reasonable that the mass complies.

Because the elite command the bulk of society's wealth and training, they usually perform their tasks very effectively. Because they possess high status and occupy most of society's positions of power, many of their decisions are accepted and carried out.

The elite who can personally impinge on society share a common view, that "from the palace," as contrasted with that of the mass, which sees society "from the public square."[1] The elite regularly interact with one another and they have common interests and values. Elites or leaders of even the most opposing groups, such as the head of the steelworkers union and the head of Inland Steel, share certain interests that differ from those of the rank and file. An example of such a common interest is maintenance of the existing order, the sustaining of a structure that permits each leader to retain his leadership.

The members of the masses are not individually significant. Their views are important only when expressed collectively. As individuals they lack significant resources of wealth and of education;[2] they also lack the security that

---

[1] The reference is from Machiavelli's *Discourses* as cited by Karl Mannheim in *Ideology and Utopia* (New York: Harvest Books, Harcourt Brace and Company, 1959), p. 63.
[2] Even if their level of goods consumption and of educational achievement equals that

permits long-range and large-scale planning and action. Without leadership they lack the capacity to organize or even to communicate with each other. Under normal circumstances, then, the mass's participation in policymaking consists only of approving or disapproving; they do not initiate. Most often their participation consists of voting for one of several candidates chosen by members of the elite, or of protesting, or possibly, of rioting.

To successfully initiate change, the mass requires direction by an alternative elite, either one that is derived from an alienated sector of the old elite or a new elite that has been able to develop because the old elite lost authority. Usually this happens when the old elite makes a series of inept decisions. The need for new leadership then becomes apparent. Even what we ordinarily call democratic decision making has been shown to consist mostly of leaders giving careful explanations of their policies; it does not involve genuine exchange, debate, or division; it involves the participants' actively giving their consent.[3] In other cultures, too, it has been shown that the fundamental requirement of democracy is "trust," "confidence," or "consent"—that is, acceptance by the mass of elite decisions.[4]

The two approaches to nonviolent resistance discussed earlier seem compatible with this description of the leaders and the led. The individual approach seems especially suited to the elite—those who lead, those who are individually effective. This is because this kind of nonviolence relies on persuasion. It is absolutely dependent on access either to officials with the capacity to effect change, or to the media and therefore to the masses who must approve change. Even if an individual elite resister does not persuade others of the need for change, he may be effective either in raising new issues or in changing the boundaries of public debate—that is, he may redefine the location of the middle of the road.

Unfortunately, even though the elite are well equipped to practice individual nonviolent resistance because of their visibility, their authority, and their resources (such as money, status, position, and education), they have a tendency not to do so. Although one might expect that those who possess the most power and authority and who are therefore most able to exercise moral leadership would feel a special obligation to call for change based on moral imperatives, they apparently do not. Many of them believe not only that they ought to be excepted from the moral code that binds non-elites, but that they ought to follow a different code because of their power.[5] Elites are as self-interested as other members of society.

The second kind of nonviolent resistance is the one the masses can use. Theirs is the view of the affected, not of the effective. Their emphasis is on

---

of the members of the elite, they do not control the kind of resources that give them power over others.

[3] See Sidney Verba, *Small Groups and Political Behavior: A Study of Leadership* (Princeton, N.J.: Princeton University Press, 1961), chap. 9.

[4] Gabriel Almond and Sidney Verba, *Civic Culture: Political Attitudes and Democracy in Five Nations* (Boston: Little Brown and Co., 1965), pp. 493, 496.

[5] See Machiavelli and Weber. Footnote 8, chap. 4.

influencing power not on commanding it. Their strength lies in their number, their persistence, their cohesiveness, and the errors or failures of the elite. Their principal method is coercion, whether noncooperation or intervention. Their justification is that the people are sovereign.

Different methods seem appropriate to different groups. Do they also effect different kinds of change? Change can involve changes in personnel, in issues debated, in policies, or in rules. Change can also be marginal or fundamental, and immediate or incremental.[6]

Individual nonviolent resistance is most likely to raise new issues and perhaps to force changes in personnel. These changes tend to be marginal although they are often immediate. They may improve a situation, but for the most part the change is merely symbolic. People feel better, but the facts of their life remain approximately the same.[7]

Group nonviolent resistance is more likely to lead to a change in policy or even to a change in the rules. This kind of change can be fundamental; power may genuinely be redistributed. Often this change is incremental, occurring slowly rather than immediately.

Different as they may be, both kinds of nonviolent resistance assume that might cannot exist independent of right. They differ only as to how right is determined. One supposes that right really does exist and that it can be known; this is the idealist view and coincides with Plato's belief that knowledge is virtue and capacity and that it ought to rule in the person of the philosopher-king. In the second approach, truth is defined pragmatically as being what most of the most concerned people believe it to be. Thus, the people who are actively involved become the sovereign. For a society to function effectively, these two concepts of right must be similar; for a society to be considered ideal they would have to be congruent.

## Democracy and Nonviolent Resistance

Democracy is an ever recurring theme in the literature of nonviolent resistance, although the relationship between the two concepts has not been fully explained. It has been briefly argued here that group nonviolence is democratic if it succeeds, at least in the sense that it must represent the will of a majority or of a majority of the concerned.[8] Because democracy is highly valued by Americans a fuller discussion now seems necessary.

The definition of democracy that modifies the majoritarian or populist concept by adding the quality of concern may do so for more than one reason. One view that might be adopted by an elitist would be to give weight to expertise.

---

[6] The word *radical* has been deliberately avoided here because it is usually associated with change that is not only fundamental but also immediate. The fact is that most often fundamental change is incremental and immediate change is only marginal.

[7] For a discussion of symbolic politics, see Murray Edelman, *Symbolic Uses of Politics* (Urbana: University of Illinois Press, 1964), and *Politics as Symbolic Action* (Chicago: Markham Publishing Co., 1971).

[8] See chap. 5, pp. 100–101.

The aim would be to achieve the "most preferable" as opposed to the "preferred by most" solution.[9] A second and different reason would be to maximize stability, by finding "the most preferred" course of action. This description of democracy sees democracy in terms of power and perceives its principal benefit as the stability it creates by facilitating peaceful change. It describes the electoral process as a way of measuring potential for violence, law as resting on the threat of violence, and voluntarily organized groups as a safety valve that help to head off spontaneous mass revolt by letting pressures surface early. Harold Nieburg summarizes this point of view by saying that a democracy risks violence; because it does, it avoids actual violence.[10]

Weighting for "intensity" is sometimes hard to justify. One reason is that accurate measurement is difficult. The danger is that the intensity of some people's feelings may go unregistered or unnoticed by the rest of society, while the intensity of others' feelings may receive immediate, wide, and sympathetic attention. In particular, the intense feelings of those who have talent, education, organizational ties, and money rarely go ignored or unnoticed. Thus, to weigh intensity is frequently to favor elites; in this case advantage is given to those who are already advantaged. Also, if intensity is extraordinary, those who seek a policy change may not only be a minority, they may be a small minority. Guerrilla warfare would represent an extreme example, but the usual estimate is that such conflict cannot be contained except with forces numbering on the order of ten to one. That means that as few as 10 per cent of the population can prevent the other 90 per cent from making and implementing policy.

Nonviolent resistance thrives on full, active, and direct participation. In these respects, it approximates direct democracy which is often theoretically preferred to representative democracy. In practice representative democracy is usually preferred because it is thought that directly democratic government cannot be run as efficiently as representative government; that it cannot be run as wisely and intelligently; and that most people do not want to concern themselves with their own governance. This explains why a nonviolent resister can claim to be behaving democratically even when he goes outside the normal or legal channels afforded by a representative government.

Even if one accepts a definition of democracy as participation, and even if one is willing to sacrifice a certain amount of expertise and/or efficiency to realize this principle, one should draw on the experience of those who have tried to practice direct democracy if one is to fully understand its implications. The Societies of Friends practice participation. They do not practice simple majoritarianism, but instead seek full agreement, yet at least some of them believe the principle of unanimity can be applied on a large scale and to political proceedings.[11] There are hazards, however; for others who have practiced par-

---

[9] For a discussion, see Willmore Kendall and George W. Carey, "The 'Intensity' Problem and Democratic Theory," *American Political Science Review* 42 (March 1968): 5–24.
[10] See H. L. Nieburg, *Political Violence* (New York: St. Martin's Press, 1969).
[11] See Francis E. Pollard, Beatrice E. Pollard, and Robert S. Pollard, *Democracy and the Quaker Method* (London: Bannisdale Press, 1949).

ticipatory democracy recognize that it, too, can be subverted by "experts," by "dedication," by a division of labor, or by endurance contests in the form of long meetings.[12]

One final way of defining democracy and democratic participation concerns the kind of democracy in which one literally shares and participates in the lives of the humblest members of society. This conception of democracy was held by Gandhi among others. According to this point of view, one's "democracy" is measured by personal life style and service given.[13] Only a few practice this kind of democracy.

If the core of democracy is consent, it would seem that government should provide for the expression of nonconsent in some way short of civil disobedience or criminality. Surely a consent theory that does not provide for nonconsent is a mockery. In the seventeenth century it was suggested that one could always emigrate. There were opportunities around the globe to begin society more or less anew, although the reality of such an opportunity was always far less than was usually implied. But why should one be bound by geography? Why cannot a new tribalism that is voluntary, uninherited, and not territorially determined be devised? For instance, what if black Americans had their choice of being U.S. citizens, of being "citizens of the world" protected directly by the U.N., or of being Liberian citizens while remaining physically in the United States? If American-owned ships can profit from foreign registry, if national corporations can benefit from incorporation under Delaware's laws, why cannot individuals have the chance to make similar kinds of choices? It seems clear that it would be wise to join a group of some minimal size, but why shouldn't "internal migration" be a real possibility for groups instead of merely a possibility of the mind for the individual? Would not this kind of development represent a genuine and complete application of consent theory?

There is one crucial way in which the theories of nonviolent resistance and democracy are alike; both are concepts that subsume a set of procedural rules and also assumptions about the results that adherence to those rules will yield. Ever since the English civil war and the Levellers' "Agreement of the People," the literature on democracy has paid simultaneous tribute to majority rule (a means of decision making) and natural rights (the assumed end product of that decision-making). Similarly, nonviolent resistance has been described both as a way of conducting a struggle and as a way of life having certain communitarian qualities. That majorities are not necessarily the best custodians of individual liberties has been eloquently argued many times, beginning with De Tocqueville's essay on the "Tyranny of the Majority"; that nonviolent resistance does not necessarily bring harmony has been shown by civil rights and antiwar demonstrations, which have frequently increased tension and have sometimes ended in disorder and disaster rather than in new understanding.

Although neither logic nor history can satisfactorily connect democracy as a means to democracy as an end, or nonviolence as a means to nonviolence

---

[12] For illustration, see Theodore Olson and Gordon Christiansen, *The Grindstone Experiment* (Toronto: Canadian Friends Service Commitee, 1966), especially chap. 2.

[13] Jawaharlal Nehru, *Toward Freedom* (New York: John Day Company, 1942), p. 189.

as an end, the opportunity to choose either the means or the ends argument provides a convenient flexibility. For example, in the name of democracy one may argue for majority rule or for minority rights, whichever suits one's purpose. A dilemma does occur when it appears certain that democracy or nonviolence as a procedure will not yield results that are democratic or nonviolent. Then one is forced to choose among (1) advocating a technique that has such intrinsic merit that it is to be followed regardless of results; (2) conditionally urging a technique because it will produce the best possible result in the long run; and (3) maintaining devotion to a principle that is an end, and an end so desirable as to justify the use of its negation in order to realize it (for example, the use of authority or tyranny to create democracy, war to yield peace, or violence to win a beloved community).

## Problems of Nonviolent Resistance

Some general problems concerning nonviolent resistance remain. One problem is the need for more investigation of the circumstances that are most appropriate to its use. It has already been noted that some advocates of nonviolence assume that because its principles are rooted in human nature, they have universal and eternal validity—even, presumably, in situations where there is a language barrier. Others, even those who have a keen sense of timing and of how best to dramatize their views, see the opportunities for successfully practicing nonviolent resistance as quite limited. Even though they may never advocate the use of violence, their advocacy of nonviolent resistance may be limited to specific and unusual situations.

A second important point concerns evaluation. To date, nonviolent resistance has been studied principally by its advocates; further, little of their analysis has been devoted to situations in which nonviolence was tried and in which it failed. Martin Luther King, Jr., had little success in Chicago. Why? Black Africans paid a high price for their resistance in South Africa, but about all that was won was a Nobel Peace Prize for Chief Luthuli. What went wrong there? What would the effect on Martin Luther King, Jr., have been if he had visited South Africa instead of India?

Another problem concerns *what* one evaluates. Ordinarily the efficacy of a campaign would be measured by comparing stated goals with accomplished goals. However, Johan Galtung, among others, has pointed out that something that is satisfying has two parameters—the instrumental and the expressive.[14] When one compares stated purposes with accomplishments one is examining only the instrumental dimension, and that this is the correct way to assess total efficacy is not at all sure. Is expressive satisfaction not just as important? Certainly the writings of Gregg, Martin Luther King, Jr., and many others emphasize the expressive value of nonviolent resistance at least as much as they do its instrumental value. Again and again King makes reference to the new dignity and self-esteem

---

[14] Johan Galtung, "Pacifism from a Sociological Point of View," *Journal of Conflict Resolution* 3 (March 1959): 67–84.

imparted to those blacks who have participated in nonviolent activity. Still, one wonders whether expressive efficacy can be sufficient or whether one must realize expressive and instrumental goals simultaneously. Also, what is to be done when one's expressive and instrumental goals interfere with one another?

Galtung believes there is more danger of losing instrumental efficacy through thoughtless concentration on achieving expressive satisfaction than vice versa. Indeed, he argues that there is a tendency to incorrectly interpret the expressive as instrumental. He illustrates this by noting that in our society the expression of violence often gives the actor a feeling of relief or of satisfaction. This feeling of satisfaction then leads him to interpret his behavior as having been instrumental whether or not his original purposes were fulfilled. Therefore, Galtung says, society would be well served if its values could be reversed so that violent activity would not give expressive satisfaction but instead would produce a feeling of shame or guilt. The same argument is made by Jerome Frank, a psychiatrist who has specialized in questions relating to war. He agrees that a reorientation of values is required, so that restraint rather than aggression is honored; so that one's peers and oneself regard the absorption of suffering rather than its infliction as manly. As a phychiatrist, Frank appreciates the complexity of human nature. Accordingly, one might suppose that he would expect such a reversal of values difficult to achieve. On the contrary, Frank's constant theme is the malleability of man; he does not doubt that such a radical alteration of values and of intellectual assumptions is both feasible and wise.[15]

A third question which must be answered is, simply, whether or not nonviolent resistance makes good sense. One can understand why a minority would not use violence against a majority that is willing to use violence. One can also see that a majority that is prepared to use violence will rarely have to use it against either a nonviolent minority or a violent minority. No problem arises in the first situation. In the second, matters can usually be handled with dispatch and without any agonizing. The majority simply puts into motion routine police and judicial procedures; violence becomes the task of specialists; one does not have to philosophize, one simply has the law enforced. Nonviolent resistance, then, seems to make the most sense for a minority, or for a majority that occupies a relatively weak position. One would therefore expect it to be used defensively more often than offensively; and one might also expect it to succeed only when the challenged majority or stronger party either is prepared to be indulgent or is only apparently the majority or the stronger party.

Another group of interesting questions left unresolved concerns the description of nonviolent resistance as ritualized conflict. First, how does such ritualization take place? How is nonviolence related to other attempts to set limits on man's barbarity, like the Geneva conventions or the Middle Ages' code of chivalry? Can such ritualization occur through conscious and rational effort or must it proceed through subconscious mechanisms? Can one adequately in a

---

15 Jerome Frank, "The Psychology of Nonviolence," *Ramparts,* January-February 1965, pp. 48–51. See bibliography for other works by Frank.

college laboratory investigate trust or in controlled experiments study love? Or is the ritualization of warfare necessarily an evolutionary phenomenon and one that occurs over so long a period of time as to become a part of man's mores without his ever consciously having created a substitute for war?

Konrad Lorenz, a German naturalist whose *On Aggression* created a stir in intellectual circles, has suggested that man's social behavior may, like his physical form, be in a state of unperceived but constant evolutionary change, and that there may be general laws governing the direction of that change. Lorenz's scientific work deals with the animal world, not that of the human. Still, the crux of his argument is that the "civilized" way in which social animals resolve conflict within the species might serve as a model for man. Lorenz notes in particular that animals with a high destructive potential who live in close association have ritualized their intraspecies contests for power. This is not done out of sympathy, tolerance, enlightened self-interest, or a desire to cooperate; it is done unconsciously and serves to preserve the species by rendering a superior-inferior verdict without necessitating a coup de grace. In one of his earlier works, *King Solomon's Ring,* Lorenz describes the typical ritualized battles that occur between wolves. Physical conflict, he notes, does occur, but when one wolf has gained a clear advantage, the other deliberately exposes his jugular vein. Because the first wolf does not take this opportunity to slay his adversary, some authors have cited this as an example of the triumph of nonviolence. However, although the loser does not die, he loses; he does not triumph. Lorenz makes it quite clear that this is a gesture of submission. The winner stands menacingly over the jugular until wearied of the whole affair and then permits the loser to steal quietly away. It is dominance—not understanding—that is established. (Or perhaps it is understanding of the dominance.)

Other questions have arisen from the practice of nonviolent resistance which have not been given answers by explanations of either individual or group resistance. One concerns the effect of combining issues in a campaign. Can one simultaneously fight war, racism, and poverty? Was Gandhi wise to try to drive out the English, end caste distinctions, and reconcile Hindu and Moslem all at once? What is the effect of separation and of combination both for the resister and for his effect on his opponent?

Another question that has been raised involves the use of children in nonviolent action. Should children be forbidden, permitted, invited, or urged to take part in protest, in civil disobedience, or in intervention? This problem was vividly illustrated in the Birmingham, Alabama, civil rights demonstrations. Hundreds of children demonstrated, were chased along country roads in automobiles, and were jailed. Children should not be asked to do adult's work; on the other hand, children do suffer from adult actions and can have an effect on them. How does one determine whether they should or should not participate? Children were attacked in Birmingham; yet the attack on them provoked such a strong public reaction that their participation clearly assisted the demonstration.

Another problem in nonviolent resistance concerns secrecy and openness. One of the chief guidelines of individual resistance is openness. Complete honesty is said to be necessary for complete communication. Thus, Quakers refer to the importance of plain speaking, and Gandhi and his followers put their names and addresses on their protest literature. This theme is not so common in the literature of group nonviolent resistance, and frequently openness is not practiced. In the Montgomery bus strike, for example, literature was left in public places, but its author was not identified and its distributor was careful not to be seen. Excessive secrecy and excessive openness are each possessed of disadvantages. The latter creates problems for effective organization, leadership, continuity, and long-range planning. Strict secrecy, on the other hand, can lead to what Jerry Rubin has described as "conservatism disguised as militancy." It also enables one's opponent to use paranoia as his weapon, when, as Rubin says, it is properly the resister's weapon.[16] One solution that has been proposed is that planning be done in secret but action be done in public.

Finally, two modifications of nonviolent resistance are proposed with some regularity. One permits the destruction of at least some kinds of property; the second permits violent self-defense. The Boston Tea Party is cited over and over again as an example of nonviolent resistance, even by persons who define nonviolence as including restraint from injury of persons or their property. Illogical as this is, it probably occurs because advocates of nonviolent resistance wish to invoke patriotism and also to illustrate the wide range of forms such resistance can take. David Dellinger and the Fathers Berrigan argue that property destruction can in some cases be nonviolent because some property (such as selective service files) "has no right to exist." This position, too, seems to contradict nonviolent principles, although it must be conceded that property destruction is preferable to human destruction, and also that human life is too often sacrificed to protect the existence of property.

In the same way, violent self-defense may seem just and reasonable. However, it also seems clearly to violate the nonviolence taboo. In addition, it exposes one to attack by those who are willing falsely to claim that *they* have acted in self-defense. Also, once defense becomes collective instead of individual, once defense becomes planned, organized, and coordinated, there is a real danger that defensive action may become initiated action and that ultimately "self-defense" will come to encompass exactly the same activities as those now encompassed by conventional military organizations.

## Criticisms of Nonviolent Resistance

It would not seem fair to end without noting that nonviolent resistance has a number of vigorous critics. First, Marxists generally regard it as a snare to the exploited, believing that those holding power will never relinquish it except when subjected to pressure by a superior power. John Lewis's *The Case Against Pacifism* is an excellent presentation of the Marxist position, and one that presents fairly and comprehensively the pacifist view that Lewis seeks to controvert. Robert Williams's *Negroes with Guns* represents a modern American

16 See Jerry Rubin, *We Are Everywhere* (New York: Harper & Row, 1971), p. 220.

black's response to the Southern civil rights movement of the late 1950s and early 1960s. Here it is argued that nonviolence is servile. Williams, who once had to go into exile in Cuba, is generally considered a Marxist, although it is not at all clear that his original position on nonviolence was derived from Marxist principles. Nor is it even clear that his Marxism was not the product of his exile rather than the reason for it.

Another argument has been made concerning the creativity and beauty of an act of violence. There is something of this in Franz Fanon's *The Wretched of the Earth*; and this is certainly part of Sorel's *Reflections on Violence*. It may well be, however, that the crucial aesthetic experience actually involves reading and writing about violence rather than participating in it. Sorel did not say, after all, that the myth of the general strike must be realized in order to be efficacious. Also, the essence of Fanon's celebration of violence may be based more on the development of the actor's sense of efficacy than on a need for "revenge." Fanon describes violence as cleansing, as unifying, and as strengthening. All these qualities can as well be associated with nonviolent resistance.

Others make an argument that the prophets of nonviolence are men who have not been tried in the crucible, that they are men who lack the knowledge or the imagination to perceive what genuine evil is like. G. C. Field and Karl Jaspers are two philosophers who hold this view.[17]

The most frequently taken position in criticism of nonviolence is that which can be traced to the various theories of a "just war." This is Miller's position; it is also the position of Howard Zinn and Reinhold Niebuhr. These men suppose, first that social life is not possible without coercion, and second, that there is no significant ethical distinction to be made between violent and nonviolent coercion if the goal is moral and the means proportional.

Finally, there are three arguments against an absolute commitment to nonviolence that have never been satisfactorily answered—at least for those whose concern is with this and not another world. The first involves the management of those individuals whom a psychiatrist would judge to be mentally ill. While mental hospitals have dramatically reduced the use of violence in their handling of patients, for reasons of principle and because of the ready availability of tranquilizers, physical restraints have not been completely forsworn. Nevertheless, a true believer in nonviolence should agree to forgo the use of violence entirely, even in the case of obvious and serious pathology, unless he is prepared to define the mentally ill as somehow "not human."[18]

The second unresolved issue concerns the potential incompatibility of

---

[17] See G. C. Field, *Pacifism and Conscientious Objection* (Cambridge, England: University Press, 1945); and Karl Jaspers, *The Future of Mankind*, trans. E. B. Ashton (Chicago: University of Chicago Press, 1961.)

[18] The case of the sadist has not been considered here because it has been suggested that a sadist would not find pleasure in hurting a nonviolent resister because the response of that person would not be to snivel and beg but to accept and to shame.

On the other hand, several gaming experiments have been cited as evidence that pacifism invites exploitation. See Anatol Rapoport, "Formal Games as Probing Tools for Investigating Behavior Motivated by Trust and Suspicion," *Journal of Conflict Resolution* 7, no. 3 (September 1963): 570–79; and Gerald H. Shure, Robert J. Meeker, and Earle A.

an ethic of noninjury with one of responsibility for seeing to the welfare of others. It may be that the answer "one can be most responsible in the long run by living the doctrine of nonviolence" is true. However, even if one has strength enough to remain nonviolent while suffering oneself or while observing other adults suffer, it would be an extraordinary discipline that could keep one from acting (if one had the resources to do so) as a protector to an abused child.[19]

A third limiting case for nonviolent resistance would seem to be when the goal of one's foe is one's annihilation.[20] In this case a resister's pledge to die "if necessary" would evoke delight, not hesitation, on the part of his opponent. The committed advocate of nonviolence would probably be wise to opt for a policy of avoidance or flight in these circumstances. He might also argue, however, that in the long run his opponent would (or at least could) understand that his real wish was different, that he did not have extinction as a primary goal.

## Conclusion

It would be nice to conclude with a message worthy of stone tablets or marble, but this discussion has raised as many questions as it has answered.

---

Hansford, "The Effectiveness of Pacifist Strategies in Bargaining Games," *Journal of Conflict Resolution* 9, no. 1 (March 1965): 106–17.

Experimental conditions are useful because they permit control of variables that cannot be controlled when one actually practices nonviolent resistance. On the other hand, the conditions that many consider necessary to such resistance may not be part of particular experiments. In the experiment referred to, for instance, there was no expectation that the relationship would be a long-term or continuing one; there was no interdependence; there was no direct contact between the contestants; there was no real "suffering" involved; there were no third-party pressures or adjunct techniques employed; and there were no intermediate or incremental steps that could be taken. Thus, an advocate of nonviolent resistance might easily claim that the experiment was not disconfirming but confirming of his views.

[19] It should also be remembered, however, that "acting on behalf of" has produced some of man's worst behavior. A sense of agency can lead one to justify brutalities one would never try to explain even on grounds of self-defense.

[20] Game theorists have tried to describe abstractly the relationship between two parties by saying that it consists of either a zero-sum game, a non-zero-sum game, or a game of pure coordination. The situation described above might be considered a zero-sum game in which the two parties have equal and opposing interests. As in checkers, one wins only if the other loses. This is the situation advocates of nonviolent resistance often refuse to face.

Resisters who advocate individual nonviolent resistance tend to perceive the world as potentially harmonious, that is, as a game of pure coordination. One profits only and as all profit, whether the task be one of fighting a forest fire or of climbing an unscaled peak. Those who advocate group nonviolent resistance would be likely to describe the world as a non-zero-sum game, as an environment with incomplete antagonism. In the general form of the non-zero-sum game the parties involved may profit or be punished unequally. Still, there is a balance point where each will maximize his profit. To reach this point, the different parties may have to exchange trust. Some would say that group nonviolence consists of a series of endeavors to reach this balance point. It would seem that everyone should be prepared to go this far with nonviolent resisters, that is, to the point where payoff coincides with power. Resistance becomes serious and is resisted, when it goes beyond trying to get the most for everyone out of the existing system, that is, when it tries to change the stakes in or the rules of the game. For a further discussion of game theory, see Anatol Rapoport, *Fights, Games and Debates* (Ann Arbor: University of Michigan Press, 1960), and Thomas Schelling, *The Strategy of Conflict* (Cambridge, Mass.: Harvard University Press, 1960).

Even if the reader now has some sense as to how and when nonviolent resistance is likely to work, he may still wonder, *"Can* I practice nonviolent resistance? *Should* I practice nonviolent resistance? *Will* I practice nonviolent resistance?

Nonviolent resistance seems to involve at least two ways of altering behavior. One of them works through individual persuasion, uses a variety of psychological devices, and requires intelligent, creative, and deft action. It seeks to reveal truth so that all can recognize it. The second method involves determined group action, or rather, reaction, for basically it responds to the proposals, plans, and actions of society's leadership. At best it rules by accepting or refusing.

The first kind of resistance is most effective when the individual is known and respected as an individual, when he fulfills vital functions in society, when he commands enough resources to be personally efficacious, when he has access to those he wishes to persuade, and when he shares the values of his opponent or can appeal to the opponent on the basis of his own values.

The second kind is used by ordinary people facing extraordinary circumstances. It requires perseverance and solidarity. It is easier if the resisters and their opponents are interdependent, if the resisters belong to a variety of independent voluntary organizations, and if they have formed stable alliances and coalitions.[21] The power exercised here is derived from society's slack.

*Can* you practice nonviolence? You will have to decide that. It has been done; it has even been done by prisoners seeking to alter the conditions of their imprisonment. The real question is what price you are willing to pay for a goal you desire. Usually one does not know the answer to this question until he has taken action. In the face of repression some quit and others go much further than they had ever envisioned. The need for practice, for action to test oneself, is one of the important and persistent themes in nonviolent literature. It cannot be overemphasized.

*Should* you engage in nonviolent resistance? As long as discrimination, poverty, unemployment, and ignorance afflict so many it seems difficult to deny the need for social change. A recent survey showed that Americans do see these ills, and also see that they produce violence and disruption. Unfortunately, the remedy for the symptoms of these social ills that most Americans choose is more and more efficient law enforcement.[22] It is true that only a fraction of the crimes committed in this country result in a conviction, and that few of these are dealt with according to our legal myths (such as trial by one's peers), but what is tragic about the public's perception and its prescription is that it seems to choose law enforcement because it sees no way to tackle these serious problems directly. The public seems to see no method that will permit it to be efficacious; it feels no capacity. It is therefore understandable why it feels no responsibility, why it cries out only for protection. Nonviolent resistance, however, *is* a form of power

---

[21] Allies seek a common purpose but have different resources and risks. Coalitions can also have different purposes, though each party agrees to help the other to its goal if the other will in turn assist him.

[22] Monica D. Blumenthal, Robert L. Kahn, Frank M. Andrews, "Attitudes Toward Violence" (unpublished paper of the Institute for Social Research, University of Michigan, 1971).

—the power of truth, of organization, and of solidarity. Because the practice of nonviolent resistance brings with it a feeling of capacity and of effectiveness, a nonviolent resister frequently becomes willing to face fundamental problems. He is less quick to demand more legal violence and more threats of legal violence. Yes, one should at least be prepared to practice nonviolent resistance.

An element important for practicing nonviolent resistance is understanding it. One must accurately perceive the link between nonviolent action and reaction to it. It is important to see such a link because often it not only goes unobserved; it is actually denied. Oftentimes those on whom resisters place pressure deny absolutely that changes in their behavior are the result of pressure. This is because they do not wish to admit that others hold power over them or can influence them. Thus officials have denied that new recreation and employment programs for ghetto youth were connected to urban riots. Similarly, deescalation of the Vietnam War has been said to be unrelated to antiwar demonstrations. This kind of denial can be destructive and alienating. Citizens who have every right to feel efficacious and loyal to their country are made to feel that they are neither.

Nonviolence requires formal and routine teaching just as violence does. At the very least, the same resources should be applied to its research and development as are applied to the cultivation of violence. Teaching of nonviolent resistance should probably be required subject matter. The goal would be to make citizens more politically effective. A government that claims to be based on consent should provide its citizens with the information and weapons necessary for nonconsent. If it does not, its claim is fraudulent.

*Will* you practice nonviolent resistance? Perhaps it will seem that the author is, like Jeremiah, trying to avert the worst by predicting it. Nevertheless, the prediction must be negative. Few of this book's readers will undertake nonviolent resistance.

This is not because the reader is immoral or opposed to change. It is because, as individuals, few readers of this book will feel effective enough to be tempted to engage in individual action, and collectively their situation will not be desperate enough to bring them to resistance. The reader is likely to be too rewarded and advantaged by the system to wish to resist it. Also, he is likely to be shielded from having to acknowledge the legal violence that is exercised on his behalf. While he is probably decent and perhaps "liberal," that is, willing to have others "catch up," he is not likely to be ready to diminish his well-being for the sake of equality. He is not likely to be ready to sacrifice.

There must be no doubt about the fact that successful nonviolent resistance does require sacrifice. The argument that it is economical does not mean that is comes cheaply. It is inexpensive only as compared with violence, but any change—even the most nonviolent—is costly. Losses will always be suffered and more losses may be suffered by the nonviolent resister than by his opponents; personally, he may even have to endure more losses than if he had used violence.

Even though the reader seems unlikely to practice nonviolent resistance, it may well be practiced on him. If it is, his response as moral judge or as agent of the elite will be important. Even if he believes himself to be un-involved he will help to determine whether or not the resistance of others suc-ceeds.

The reader should recognize quite clearly both his privilege and the many varieties of violence—legal and illegal—that secure his privilege. He should not commend nonviolence to others if he is not willing to rely on it himself.[23] He should recognize, too, the dishonesty involved in endorsing violence in foreign affairs and nonviolence at home.

This is essentially a liberal argument. It is intellectual and it is in-cremental. It says to the reader in essence, "Let needed change occur" rather than "Go forth and make change." This is probably a morally indefensible posi-tion. It may, however, be the most that can be hoped for. People can sometimes be induced to sacrifice their expectations; they can rarely be persuaded to give up their current comforts.

If readers of this book are willing to commit themselves to regular, incremental change in the direction of justice and if they will refuse to act as oppressors for the elite, much will be accomplished. If they are ready to make genuine sacrifices and to work for justice itself, the author will be greatly but pleasantly surprised.[24]

---

[23] Jerry Rubin comments on this point that "the pacifists, most of whom are white liberal middle-class intellectuals, have got to start preaching pacifism to the White House, Pentagon, and police departments, not to the Panthers and Weatherpeople." *We Are Everywhere*, p. 200.

[24] A chief limit on an individual's commitment to sacrificial work is those who are directly dependent on him, in particular, his children. This means that those who are both non-dependent and without dependents would seem to have a special opportunity to work for social change. In our society this would involve two groups: those from perhaps 18 to 24 and those over 50 or 60. An alliance between these groups is one that has been little considered although it may now be emerging in ecology organizations.

# Epilogue

Although I have always been attracted by persons whose views are uncomplicated and who can wholeheartedly involve themselves in action, although Tom Paine, John Brown, and Carrie Nation rank among my favorite heroes and heroines, I have not been gifted with their "one-eyed" vision nor with their capacity for violence. Still I am not "persuaded" to nonviolence either. I should like to believe as the group nonviolent strategist believes, but I do not feel I can advocate nonviolence for others while occupying a position of privilege. Unless one shares the plight of the oppressed, one should not preach to them. To me, Abe Fortas's resignation from the Supreme Court was as much required by his sermon on civil disobedience as it was by his financial and political activities.

I hope this discussion will assist those working for social change— that they will learn to be more creative, more effective, and more enduring. I hope, too, that America's educated and comfortable will better recognize that any discussion of violence must include the violence that is legal and also that which is illegal but officially permitted. It should be clear that Daniel Moynihan is insulting and perhaps even maligning when he addresses a student audience on the dangers of campus violence but refuses to discuss the war in Vietnam (University of Wisconsin, Spring 1969).

Finally, I would argue that neither cynicism nor apathy is appropriate for those who wish social change. Nonviolent protest and resistance can be potent. They can initiate change by dramatically raising unasked questions, by persuading the established, and by arousing the public to force fundamental change. The cynic degrades his fellowmen; the apathetic degrades himself. At the very least, a form of Pascal's wager applies: to endeavor may yield dividends; not to endeavor guarantees failure.

# Selected Bibliography

This bibliography has two purposes. The first is to provide a record of sources used in preparing this volume. The second is to suggest how a student interested in exploring nonviolence more fully might begin such a study. Thus, works that the author considers fundamental or especially insightful have been marked with an asterisk (*). In the last section, a number of recent works are listed including some that do not discuss nonviolence per se. Indeed, they tend to focus either on violence or on resistance to war. This reflects two trends: first, violent civil disturbances apparently increased from 1960 to 1970; and second, antiwar activity, while mostly nonviolent, did not always describe itself as nonviolent. Although these last-mentioned works were not used in preparing this volume, they are of importance to the serious student.

## General Works on Nonviolent Resistance

### Books and Pamphlets

American Friends Service Committee. *An Introduction to the American Friends Service Committee.* Philadelphia: n.p., 1962.

American Society of Friends Service Committee. *Speak Truth to Power.* Philadelphia: n.p., 1956.

*Analysis of Nonviolence in Theory and Fact.* Special issue of *Sociological Inquiry* 38 (Winter 1968).

Asinof, Eliot. *Craig and Joan: Two Lives for Peace.* New York: Viking Press, 1971.

Ballou, Adin. *Non-Resistance in Relation to Human Governments.* Boston: Non-resistance Society, 1839.

Bell, Inge Powell. *CORE and the Strategy of Nonviolence.* New York: Random House, 1968.

*Bigelow, Albert. *The Voyage of the Golden Rule.* Garden City, N.Y.: Doubleday & Co., 1959.

*Bondurant, Joan. *Conquest of Violence. The Gandhian Philosophy of Conflict.* Rev. ed. Berkeley, Cal.: University of California Press, 1965.

Carter, April. *Direct Action.* London: Peace News, 1962.

Carter, April, David Hoggett, and Adam Roberts. *Non-violent Action: A Selected Bibliography*. London: Housmans, 1966.

Case, Clarence M. *Non-Violent Coercion*. New York: Century Co., 1923.

*Civilian Defense*. London: Peace News, 1964.

Curti, Merle. *Peace or War*. New York: W. W. Norton & Co., 1936.

Day, Dorothy. *Loaves and Fishes*. New York: Harper & Row, 1963.

————. *The Long Loneliness*. New York: Harper & Brothers, 1952.

*Deming, Barbara. *Prison Notes*. New York: Grossman Publishers, 1966.

*Dunn, Ted, ed. *Alternatives to War and Violence*. London: J. Clarke, 1963.

Fanon, Franz. *The Wretched of the Earth*. New York: Grove Press, 1968.

*Farmer, James. *Freedom, When?* New York: Random House, 1965.

Finn, James, ed. *Protest: Pacifism and Politics*. New York: Random House, Vintage Books, 1968.

*Gandhi, M. K. *Non-Violent Resistance*. New York: Schocken Books, 1951.

Glover, Edward. *War, Sadism and Pacifism*. London: G. Allen & Unwin, 1935.

Gregg, Richard. *A Discipline for Nonviolence*. Pendle Hill Pamphlet no. 11. Wallingford, Pa., 1935.

————. *Pacifist Program in Time of War, Threatened War or Fascism*. Pendle Hill Pamphlet no. 5. Wallingford, Pa., 1939.

*————. *The Power of Nonviolence*. Rev. ed. Nyack, N.Y.: Fellowship Publications, 1962.

————. *The Psychology and Strategy of Gandhi's Nonviolent Resistance*. Madras: n.p., 1929.

————. *The Self Beyond Yourself*. Philadelphia: J. B. Lippincott Co., 1956.

————. *Spirit Through Body*. Boston: University Press, 1956.

————. *The Value of Voluntary Simplicity*. Pendle Hill Pamphlet no. 3. Wallingford, Pa., 1934.

*Hare, A. Paul and Herbert H. Blumberg, eds. *Nonviolent Direct Action*. Washington: Corpus Books, 1968.

Hentoff, Nat. *Peace Agitator—The Story of A. J. Muste*. New York: Macmillan Co., 1963.

Holmes, John Haynes. *I Speak for Myself*. New York: Harper & Brothers, 1959.

————. *New Wars for Old*. New York: Dodd, Mead and Co., 1918.

*James, William. *The Moral Equivalent of War*. London: Peace News, 1963.

Jaspers, Karl. *The Future of Mankind*. Translated by E. B. Ashton. Chicago: University of Chicago Press, 1961.

King, Martin Luther, Jr. *Strength to Love*. New York: Harper & Row, 1963.

*————. *Stride Toward Freedom*. New York: Harper & Brothers, 1958.

————. *Where Do We Go from Here: Chaos or Community?* New York: Bantam Books, 1968.

————. *Why We Can't Wait*. New York: Harper & Row, 1964.

King-Hall, Stephen. *Power Politics in the Nuclear Age*. London: Gollancz, 1962.

Kuper, Leo. *Passive Resistance in South Africa*. New Haven: Yale University Press, 1957.

La Boétie, Etienne. *Anti-Dictator*. New York: Columbia University Press, 1942.

Lakey, George *Nonviolent Action: How It Works.* Pendle Hill Pamphlet no. 129. Wallingford, Pa., 1963.

Lewis, John. *The Case Against Pacifism.* London: George Allen and Unwin, 1937.

Lynd, Staughton, ed. *Nonviolence in America: A Documentary History.* New York: Bobbs-Merrill, American Heritage Series, 1966.

Martin, David. *Pacifism.* London: Routledge & Kegan Paul, 1965.

*Mayer, Peter, ed. *The Pacifist Conscience.* London: Pelican Books, 1966.

*Miller, William. *Nonviolence.* New York: Schocken Books, 1966.

*Naess, Arne. *Gandhi and the Nuclear Age.* Totowa, N.J.: Bedminster Press, 1965.

*Olson, Theodore and Gordon Christiansen. *The Grindstone Experiment.* Toronto: Canadian Friends Service Committee, 1966.

*Oppenheimer, Martin and George Lakey. *A Manual for Direct Action.* Chicago: Quadrangle Books, 1964.

Peck, James. *We Who Would Not Kill.* New York: Stuart, 1958.

Pollard, Francis E., Beatrice E. Pollard, and Robert S. W. Pollard. *Democracy and the Quaker Method.* London: Bannisdale Press, 1949.

*Ramachandran, G. and T. K. Mahadevan, eds. *Gandhi: His Relevance for Our Times.* Bombay: Bharatiya Vidya Bhavan, 1964.

Ramsey, Paul. *Christian Ethics and the Sit-In.* New York: Association Press, 1961.

Reynolds, Earle. *The Forbidden Voyage.* New York: D. McKay Co., 1961.

*Roberts, Adam, ed. *The Strategy of Civilian Defense.* London: Faber and Faber, 1967.

Robertson, D. B., ed. *Love and Justice.* Philadelphia: Westminster Press, 1957.

Scott, Michael. *A Time to Speak.* Garden City, N.Y.: Doubleday & Co., 1958. (View of a white living in South Africa.)

*Seifert, Harvey. *Conquest by Suffering.* Philadelphia: Westminster Press, 1965.

Sharp, Gene. *Creative Conflict in Politics.* London: Housmans, 1962.

*————. *Exploring Nonviolent Alternatives.* Boston: Porter Sargent, 1970.

————. *Gandhi Faces the Storm.* Ahmedabad: Navajivan Publishing House, 1961.

————. *Gandhi Wields the Weapons of Moral Power.* Ahmedabad: Navajivan Publishing House, 1960.

————. *Nonviolent Action.* London: Peace News, 1963.

————. *The Political Equivalent of War—Civilian Defense: International Conciliation,* no. 555, November 1965.

*————. *The Politics of Nonviolent Action.* Center for International Affairs, Harvard University, August 1966 (copy one), and April 1968 (copy two). (Mimeographed) To be published by Pilgrim Press, 1505 Race Street, Philadelphia.

————. *Tyranny Could Not Quell Them.* London: Peace News, 1954.

Sharp, Gene, T. K. Mahadevan, and Adam Roberts, eds. *Civilian Defense.* Bombay: Bharatiya Vidya Bhavan, 1967.

*Shridharani, Krishnalal. *War Without Violence*. Bombay: Bharatiya Vidya Bhavan, 1962.

Sibley, Mulford. *Unilateral Initiatives and Disarmament*. Beyond Deterrence Series. American Friends Service Committee. Philadelphia, 1962.

*Sibley, Mulford Q., ed. *The Quiet Battle*. Garden City, N.Y.: Doubleday & Co., Anchor Books, 1963.

Sibley, Mulford and Philip E. Jacob. *Conscription of Conscience*. Ithaca, N.Y.: Cornell University Press, 1952.

Smith, Lillian. *Our Faces, Our Words*. New York: W. W. Norton & Co., 1964. (Deals with Southern civil rights movement.)

Sorel, George. *Reflections on Violence*. New York: Collier Press, 1961.

Sorokin, Pitirim. *The Ways and Power of Love*. Boston: Beacon Press, 1954.

Sorokin, Pitirim, ed. *Forms and Techniques of Altruistic and Spiritual Growth*. Boston: Beacon Press, 1954.

Templin, Ralph. *Democracy and Nonviolence*. Boston: Porter Sargent, 1965.

Thurman, Howard. *The Luminous Darkness*. New York: Harper & Row, 1965.

Tolstoy, Leo. *Letter to a Hindu*. London: Peace News, 1963.

———. *The Kingdom of God is Within You*. New York: Noonday Press, 1961.

———. *The Law of Violence and the Law of Love*. London: Westminster Press, 1959.

Walker, Charles C. *Organizing for Nonviolent Direct Action*. Cheyney, Pa.: by the author, 1961.

*Waskow, Arthur I. *From Race Riot to Sit-In*. Garden City, N.Y.: Doubleday & Co., 1966.

Weinberg, Arthur and Lila Weinberg, eds. *Instead of Violence*. Boston: Beacon Press, 1963.

## Articles in Journals

Frank, Jerome. "Breaking the Thought Barrier: Psychological Challenges of the Nuclear Age." *Psychiatry* 23 (August 1960): 245–66.

———. "The Psychology of Nonviolence." *Ramparts*, January-February 1965, pp. 48–51.

*Galtung, Johan. "Pacifism from a Sociological Point of View." *Journal of Conflict Resolution* 3 (March 1959): 67–84.

Hentoff, Nat. "By Common Dissent." *Commonwealth*, January 19, 1962, pp. 433–35.

Leonard, Edward A. "Ninety-Four Years of Non-Violence." *New South*, April 1965, pp. 3–6.

Lippmann, Walter. "The Political Equivalent of War." *Atlantic Monthly*, August 1928, pp. 181–87.

Mabee, Carleton. "Evolution of Nonviolence." *Nation*, August 12, 1961, pp. 78–81.

Mazrui, Ali. "Sacred Suicide." *Atlas*, March 1966, pp. 164–69.

*Miller, William. "A Select Bibliography of Notable Books for Pacifists." *Fellowship* 26 (March 1, 1960): 21–24.

————. "Nonviolence in the Racial Crisis." *Christian Century,* July 22, 1964, pp. 927–30.

————. "Peace-Making and Peace-Keeping." *Gandhi Marg,* April 1966, n.p.

————. "Problems of Nonviolence." *Fellowship,* July 1, 1961, p. 15 ff.

————. "Protest and Constructive Peace Action." *Gandhi Marg,* n.d., n.p.

————. "Socialism and the Open Heart." *Gandhi Marg,* n.d., n.p.

————. "The Lesser Evil and the Least." *Fellowship,* November 1, 1958, pp. 9–12.

Naess, Arne. "A System of Gandhian Ethics of Conflict Resolution." *Journal of Conflict Resolution* 2 (June 1958): 140–55.

*Narreson, Jan. "Pacifism: A Philosophical Analysis." *Ethics* 75 (July 1965): 259–71.

*Nieburg, H. L. "The Threat of Violence and Social Change." *American Political Science Review* 56 (December 1962): 865–73.

Oppenheimer, Martin. "Towards a Sociological Understanding of Nonviolence." *Sociological Inquiry* 35 (Winter 1965): 123–31.

Sharp, Gene. "A South African Contribution to the Study of Nonviolent Action: A Review." Review of *Passive Resistance in South Africa* by Leo Kuper. *Journal of Conflict Resolution* 5 (December 1961): 395–402.

————. "Beyond World Government." *Peace News* (London, February 28, 1964), pp. 6–7.

————. "Britain Considers Her Weapons." *Gandhi Marg* 3 (April 1959), n.p.

————. "Can Nonviolence Work in South Africa?" *Peace News* (London), June 21, 1963, n.p.

————. "Civil Disobedience in a Democracy." *Peace News* (London), February 1963, n.p.

————. "Dilemmas of Morality in Politics." *Reconciliation Quarterly* (London), no. 128 (1965), pp. 528–35. Full manuscript titled "Morality: Politics and Political Technique" (unpublished).

————. "Ethics and Responsibility in Politics." *Inquiry* (Oslo) 7 (July 1964): 304–17.

————. "Freedom and Revolution." Review of *On Revolution* by Hannah Arendt. *Peace News,* February 14, 1964, pp. 6–8.

————. "Gandhi on the Theory of Voluntary Servitude." *Gandhi Marg,* 6 (October 1962): 332–46.

————. "Gandhi's Defense Policy." *Gandhi Marg* 10 (July and October, 1966): 184–95, 249–50, 303–17.

————. "How Do You Get Rid of Oppression?" *Peace News,* October 25, 1963, n.p.

————. "India's Lessons for the Peace Movement." *Gandhi Marg,* n.d., n.p.

————. "Problems of Violent and Non-Violent Struggle." *Peace News* (London), June 28, 1963, n.p.

————. "Research Project on Totalitarianism and Nonviolent Resistance." *Journal of Conflict Resolution* 3 (June 1959): 153–61.

————. "Strategic Problems of South African Resistance." *Peace News* (London), July 5, 1963, n.p.

————. "The Meanings of Nonviolence: A Typology." *Journal of Conflict Resolution* 3 (March 1959): 41–46. (Revised version in *Gandhi Marg* 3 October 1959).

————. "The Need for a Functional Equivalent of War." *International Relations* (London) 3 (April 1967): 187–207.

Sharp, Gene with Johan Galtung. "Unarmed Strategy: Notes on Research and Analysis of Nonviolent Struggle." *Mankind* 3 (August 1958): 1–11.

Sibley, Mulford. "Revolution and Violence." *Peace News* reprint, n.d.

Thernstrom, Stephen. "The New Pacifism." *Dissent,* Autumn 1960, pp. 373–76.

Tucker, Robert. "Nuclear Pacifism." *New Republic,* February 6, 1961, pp. 19–24.

Walzer, Michael. "The Idea of Resistance." *Dissent,* Autumn 1960, pp. 369–373.

————. "The Politics of the New Negro." *Dissent,* Summer 1960, pp. 235–44.

Zinn, Howard. "The Force of Nonviolence." *Nation,* May 17, 1962, pp. 227–33.

## Journals

*Catholic Worker.*
*Dissent.*
*Ethics.*
*Fellowship.*
*Freedomways.*
*Gandhi Marg.*
*Journal of Conflict Resolution.*
*Journal of Peace Research* (Oslo).
*Liberation.*
*Peace News* (London).
*Peace Research Abstracts Journal* (Canada).
*Pendle Hill Pamphlets.*
*Win.*

# Works Related to Nonviolent Resistance

## Books and Pamphlets

Alinsky, Saul D. *Reveille for Radicals.* New York: Random House, Vintage Books, 1969.

*Arendt, Hannah. *On Violence.* New York: Harcourt, Brace & World, 1970.

*Belfarge, Sally. *Freedom Summer.* New York: Viking Press, 1965.

Bennett, Lerone, Jr. *The Negro Mood.* Chicago: Johnson Publishing Co., 1964.

*————. *What Manner of Man.* Chicago: Johnson Publishing Co., 1964. (Biography of Martin Luther King, Jr.)

Boulding, Kenneth. *Conflict and Defense.* New York: Harper & Brothers, 1962.

Brehm, Jack W. and Arthur R. Cohen. *Explorations in Cognitive Dissonance.* New York: John Wiley & Sons, 1962.

Brinton, Howard. *Friends for Three Hundred Years.* New York: Harper & Brothers, 1952.

Buss, Arnold. *The Psychology of Aggression.* New York: John Wiley & Sons, 1961.

Carthy, J. David and F. J. Ebling, eds. *The Natural History of Aggression.* New York: Published for the Institute of Biology by Academic Press, 1964.

Coser, Lewis. *The Functions of Social Conflict.* Glencoe, Ill.: Free Press of Glencoe, 1956.

Fischer, Louis. *The Life of Mahatma Gandhi.* New York: Harper & Brothers, 1950.

Frank, Jerome. *Sanity and Survival.* New York: Random House, Vintage Books, 1968.

*Gamson, William A. *Power and Discontent.* Homewood, Ill.: Dorsey Press, 1968.

Gandhi, M. K. *Gandhi's Autobiography.* Washington, D.C.: Public Affairs Press, 1948.

Goodspeed, D. J. *The Conspirators: A Study of the Coup d'Etat.* New York: Viking Press, 1962.

Group for the Advancement of Psychiatry. *Psychiatric Aspects of the Nuclear War* 5, report No. 57 (September 1964).

Hiller, E. T. *The Strike.* Chicago: University of Chicago Press, 1928.

Jameson, A. K. *Unarmed Against Fascism.* London: Peace News, 1963.

*Jouvenel, Bertrand de. *On Power.* Boston: Beacon Press, 1962.

*Katz, Robert L. *Empathy—Its Nature and Use.* New York: Free Press, 1963.

Levy, Charles J. *Voluntary Servitude.* New York: Appleton-Century-Crofts, 1968.

Lomax, Louis. *The Negro Revolt.* New York: New American Library Signet Books, 1964.

Lorenz, Konrad. *King Solomon's Ring.* New York: Crowell, 1952.

*————. *On Aggression.* New York: Harcourt, Brace & World, 1966.

Luthuli, Albert. *Let My People Go.* Johannesburg: Collins, 1962.

Luttwak, Edward. *Coup d'Etat.* Greenwich, Conn.: Fawcett Publications, 1969.

*McNeil, Elton B. ed. *The Nature of Human Conflict.* Englewood Cliffs, N.J.: Prentice-Hall, 1965.

Mehrabian, Albert. *Tactics of Social Influence.* Englewood Cliffs, N.J.: Prentice-Hall, 1970.

Mendelsohn, Jack. *The Martyrs.* New York: Harper & Row, 1966.

Nehru Jawaharlal. *Toward Freedom.* New York: John Day Co., 1942.

Peck, James. *Cracking the Color Line*. New York: CORE, 1960.

————. *Freedom Ride*. New York: Simon and Schuster, 1962.

Proudfoot, Merrill. *Diary of a Sit-In*. Chapel Hill: University of North Carolina Press, 1962.

Ramsey, Paul. *War and the Christian Conscience*. Durham, N.C.: Duke University Press, 1961.

*Rapoport, Anatol. *Fights, Games, and Debates*. Ann Arbor: University of Michigan Press, 1960.

Rose, Arnold M., ed. *The Negro Protest. Annals of the American Academy of Political and Social Science* 357. Philadelphia: January 1965.

Ruskin, John. *Unto This Last*. New York: J. Wiley & Son, 1872.

Scheler, Max. *The Nature of Sympathy*. London: Routledge & Kegan Paul, 1954.

*Schelling, Thomas. *The Strategy of Conflict*. Cambridge, Mass.: Harvard University Press, 1960.

Seed, Philip. *The Psychological Problem of Disarmament*. London: Housmans, 1966.

*Stewart, David A. *Preface to Empathy*. New York: Philosophical Library, 1956.

Sutherland, Elizabeth, ed. *Letters from Mississippi*. New York: McGraw-Hill Book Co., 1965.

Von Hoffman, Nicholas. *Mississippi Notebook*. New York: David White Co., 1964.

Waltz, Kenneth M. *Man, the State, and War*. New York: Columbia University Press, 1959.

Warren, Robert Penn. *Who Speaks for the Negro?* New York: Random House, 1965.

Williams, Robert F. *Negroes with Guns*. New York: Marzani & Munsell, 1962.

Wolfgang, Marvin, ed. *Patterns of Violence. Annals of the American Academy of Political and Social Science* 364. Philadelphia: March 1966.

Wright, Quincy, William M. Evan, and Morton Deutsch, eds. *Preventing World War III*. New York: Simon and Schuster, 1962.

*Zinn, Howard. *SNCC, The New Abolitionists*. Boston: Beacon Press, 1964.

## Articles in Journals

Finch, Roy. "The New Peace Movement." *Dissent*, Winter 1963, pp. 86–95.

Frank, Jerome. "Group Psychology and the Elimination of War." *International Journal of Group Psychiatry* 14 (January 1964): 41–48.

————. "The Great Antagonism." *Atlantic Monthly*, November 1958.

Ginsberg, Alan. "Berkeley Vietnam Days." *Liberation*, January 1966, pp. 42–43.

Janis, Irving L. and Daniel Katz. "The Reduction of Inter-Group Hostility: Research Problems and Hypotheses." *Journal of Conflict Resolution* 3 (March 1959): 85–100.

Waskow, A. I. "Why I Went to Jail." *Saturday Review of Literature*, August 24, 1963, pp. 32–33.

## Works on Civil Disobedience or Conscientious Objection

### Books and Pamphlets

Bedau, Adam, ed. *Civil Disobedience.* New York: Pegasus, 1969.

*Civil Disobedience.* Santa Barbara: Center for the Study of Democratic Institutions, April 1966.

*Cohen, Carl. *Civil Disobedience.* New York: Columbia University Press, 1971.

*Field, G. C. *Pacifism and Conscientious Objection.* Cambridge: The University Press, 1945.

Fortas, Abe. *Concerning Dissent and Civil Disobedience.* New York: New American Library, Signet Books, 1968.

Goldwin, Robert A. *On Civil Disobedience: American Essays, Old and New.* Chicago: Rand McNally, 1969.

Lynd, Alice, ed. *We Won't Go.* Boston: Beacon Press, 1968.

Plato. *Euthyphro, Crito, Apology and Symposium.* Chicago: Henry Regnery Co., 1953.

Schlissel, Lillian, ed. *Conscience in America.* New York: E. P. Dutton & Co., 1968.

*Thoreau, Henry David. *Walden or, Life in the Woods and On the Duty of Civil Disobedience.* New York: New American Library of World Literature, 1960.

Urquhart, Clara, ed. *A Matter of Life.* Boston: Little, Brown and Co., 1963.

Zinn, Howard. *Disobedience and Democracy.* New York: Random House, Vintage Books, 1968.

### Articles in Books

*Bay, Christian. "Civil Disobedience: Prerequisite for Democracy in Mass Society." *Political Theory and Social Change.* Edited by David Spitz. New York: Atherton Press, 1967.

*Walzer, Michael. "The Obligation to Disobey." *Political Theory and Social Change.* Edited by David Spitz. New York: Atherton Press, 1967.

### Articles in Journals

Cohen, Carl. "Civil Disobedience." *Nation* 148 (March 16, 1964): 257–62.

————. "The Case of Selective Pacifism." *Nation,* July 8, 1968, pp. 11–15.

*Dworkin, Ronald. "Civil Disobedience: The Case Against Prosecution." *New York Review of Books* 10 (June 6, 1968): 14–21.

Frankel, Charles. "Is It Ever Right to Break the Law?" *New York Times Magazine,* June 12, 1964, p. 17 ff.

Hunter, Allan A. "Genuine or Phony Conscience." *Christian Century,* February 13, 1952, pp. 188–89.

*Pitkin, Hanna. "Obligation and Consent." *American Political Science Review* 59 and 60 (December 1965, and March 1966) : 990–99 and 39–52.

*Pranger, Robert J. "An Explanation for Why Final Political Authority is Necessary." *American Political Science Review* 60 (December 1966) : 994–97.

*Prosch, Harry. "Limits to the Moral Claim in Civil Disobedience." *Ethics* 75 (January 1965) : 103–11.

*Rucker, Darnell. "The Moral Grounds of Civil Disobedience." *Ethics* 76 (January 1966) : 142–45.

Schwarz, Wolfgang. "The Right of Resistance." *Ethics* 74 (January 1964) : 126–34.

Spitz, David. "Democracy and the Problem of Civil Disobedience." *American Political Science Review* 48 (June 1954) : 386–403.

## Recent Works Related to Nonviolent Resistance

Anderson, Walt, ed. *The Age of Protest.* Pacific Palisades, Cal.: Goodyear Publishing Co., 1969.

Berrigan, Daniel, S. J. and Robert Coles. *The Geography of Faith.* Boston: Beacon Press, 1971.

Bieneu, Henry. *Violence and Social Change.* Chicago: University of Chicago Press, 1968.

Blumenthal, Monica D., Robert L. Kahn, Frank M. Andrews, and Kendra B. Head. *Justifying Violence: Attitudes of American Men.* Ann Arbor: Institute for Social Research.

Brock, Peter. *Pacifism in the United States: From the Colonial Era to the First World War.* Princeton, N.J.: Princeton University Press, 1968.

———. *Twentieth Century Pacifism.* New York: Van Nostrand Reinhold Co., 1970.

Cohen, Jerry and William S. Murphy. *Burn, Baby, Burn. The Los Angeles Race Riot, August, 1965.* New York: Avon, 1966.

Daly, Charles U., ed. *Urban Violence.* Chicago: University of Chicago Press, 1969.

Dellinger, David. *Revolutionary Nonviolence.* Garden City, N.Y.: Doubleday & Co., Anchor Books, 1971.

Drinan, Robert F. *Vietnam and Armageddon: Peace, War, and the Christian Conscience.* New York: Sheed and Ward, 1970. (See annotated bibliography.)

Erikson, Erik. *Gandhi's Truth.* New York: W. W. Norton & Co., 1969.

Ferber, Michael and Staughton Lynd. *The Resistance.* Boston: Beacon Press, 1971.

Goodman, Mitchell. *The Movement Toward a New America.* Philadelphia: Pilgrim Press, 1970.

Graham, Hugh Davis and Ted Robert Gurr. *Violence in America.* New York: New American Library, Signet Books, 1969.

Gray, J. Glenn. *The Warriors, Relfections on Men in Battle.* New York: Harper & Row, 1969.

———. *On Understanding Violence Philosophically.* New York: Harper & Row, 1970.

Gurr, Ted Robert. *Why Men Rebel.* Princeton, N.J.: Princeton University Press, 1970.

Hersey, John. *The Algiers Motel Incident.* New York: Bantam Books, 1968.

Horsburgh, H. J. N. *Nonviolence and Aggression.* New York: Oxford University Press, 1968.

Mabee, Carleton. *Black Freedom. The Nonviolent Abolitionists from 1830 Through the Civil War.* Toronto: Macmillan Co., 1970.

Megargee, Edwin and Jack Hokanson, eds. *The Dynamics of Aggression: Individual, Group and International Analyses.* New York: Harper & Row, 1970.

National Advisory Commission on Civil Disorders. *Report* (The Kerner Report). Washington, D.C.: U.S. Government Printing Office, 1968.

National Commission on the Causes and Prevention of Violence. *Shoot-Out in Cleveland.* New York: Bantam Books, 1969.

Oppenheimer, Martin, *The Urban Guerrilla.* Chicago: Quadrangle Books, 1969.

Rose, Thomas, ed. *Violence in America: A Historical Reader.* New York: Random House, 1970.

Shaffer, Jerome A., ed. *Violence.* New York: David McKay, 1971.

Skolnick, Jerome. *The Politics of Protest.* New York: Ballantine Books, 1969.

Toch, Hans H. *Violent Men: An Inquiry into the Psychology of Violence.* Chicago: Aldine Publishing Co., 1970.

*Urban Riots: Violence and Social Change. Proceedings of the Academy of Political Science* 29 (July, 1968).

Veysey, Laurence, ed. *Law and Resistance.* New York: Harper & Row, 1970.

Walter, E. V. *Terror and Resistance: A Study of Political Violence.* New York: Oxford University Press, 1969.

Walzer, Michael. *Obligations.* Cambridge, Mass.: Harvard University Press, 1970.

Wasserstrom, Richard A., ed. *War and Morality.* Belmont, Cal.: Wadsworth Publishing Co., 1970.

Wittner, Lawrence. *Rebels Against War. The American Peace Movement, 1941–1960.* New York: Columbia University Press, 1969.

# Index

Abolitionists, 18
  Civil War, 7
  pre-Civil War, 5
Action
  as mode of thought, 50
  power of, 57
  as self-discipline, 51
Action techniques, nonviolent
  economic boycott, 15
  march on Washington, 11,
    15–16
  rent strikes, 16
  restaurant sit-ins, 14
  sit-in strikes, 11
  student sit-ins, 14–15
Addams, Jane, 7, 8
*Agape,* 86
Age groups of potential protesters, 116*n*
Aggression, 21, 22
  Freud on, 58
  Lorenz on, 110
Aims of nonviolence
  to earn respect of others, 38,
    40–41
  to pay respect for others,
    38–39
  to strengthen self-respect,
    38, 39
Albany, Georgia, 15, 55–56
Alinsky, Saul, 82*n*
Allport, Gordon, 45*n*
America
  beginning of nonviolent re-
    sistance in, 3–5
  cases of nonviolent resis-
    tance in, 1–3
  civil rights organizations in,
    12, 13–16
  during Civil War, 5–7
  labor movement in, 10–11
  peace groups in, 12–13
  revolution in, 92
  suffragettes in, 9–10
  during World War I, 8–9
American Anti-Slavery Society,
  5
American Civil Liberties
  Union (ACLU), 8*n*
American Friends Service
  Committee, 12
American Peace Society, 7, 8
Americus, Georgia, 55
Amitology, 40
Anarchism, of individual nonviolent resistance, 100, 102

Arendt, Hannah, 66, 71
Atomic testing, resistance to,
  54–55
Audience, role of, 72–73
Austin, John, 66
Authority, as form of power,
  65–66

Backlash, 47
Badiali, Craig, 49*n*
Ballou, Adin, 6–7
Bargaining, and coercion, 26
Barnard, Jessie, 66
Bateson, Gregory, 42
Bell, Inge, 14
Bentham, Jeremy, 86
Berrigan, David, 111
Berrigan, Phillip, 20*n*, 111
Bigelow, Albert, 2*n,* 54
Birmingham, Alabama, 15,
  110
Blacks
  civil rights of, 7
  economic boycott by, 15
  Niebuhr on, 11
Boétie, Etienne de la, 60, 65
Bondurant, Joan, 82, 100
Boston Tea Party, 4–5, 111
Boycott, 77
Brinton, Crane, 91–92
Brown, John, 24–25, 117
Bryan, William Jennings, 7, 8
Burritt, Elihu, 7
Buses
  boycott of, 92–93
  integration of interstate, 14
  strike against in Montgom-
    ery, 14

Carnegie, Andrew, 8
Carnegie Endowment, 8
*Case Against Pacifism, The,*
  111
Catholic Worker Movement,
  12
Cause and effect, 39–40
Central Committee for Con-
  scientious Objectors, 12
Chaney, Benjamin, 16
Chaney, James, 16
Change, kinds of, 105
Chicago
  restaurant sit-ins in, 14
  school boycott in, 16
Chicago Seven, 76*n*

Children, in civil disobedience,
  110
Christian realism, 87
Christianity, and nonviolence,
  20, 85–88
Civil disobedience, 23–25,
  27–28
  and the just war, 89–90
  by suffragettes, 10
Civilians, organization of, 83
Civil rights groups, 12, 13–17
Civil War, American, 5–7, 9
Clausewitz, General von, 64
Coercion, 64
  analyzed, 19–21
  and bargaining, 26
  group vs. individual theo-
    ries of, 102, 105
  intervention as, 79
  not part of nonviolent re-
    sistance, 44–45
  Seifert on, 95
Cognitive dissonance, 45, 57
Cold war
  peace groups during, 12
  as ritualization ,100
Combined forms of nonviolent
  resistance, 33, 85–102; *see
  also* Group nonviolent resistance; Individual nonviolent resistance
  Christian position, 85–88
  civil disobedience and a just
    war, 89–90
  contrasting explanations,
    97–102
  examples of, 94–97
  revolution and, 90–92
  tactical, 88–89
  tactics of, 92–94
Commitment, and power of
  consent, 68–69
Committee for Non-Violent
  Action Against Nuclear
  Weapons (CNVA), 1
Committee for Nonviolent Action, 12
Communication
  by action, 50
  as goal of protest, 77
  non-verbal, 48, 50
  openness of, 110–11
  verbal, 48
Communists, in peace movement, 12
Comte, Auguste, 65–66

129

Conflict
  group vs. individual theories
    of, 102
  inherent in social life, 61
  objections to theory of,
    61–62
Congress of Racial Equality
  (CORE), 8n, 13–14, 15,
  16, 81, 84
Conquest by Suffering, 94
Conscience, 90, 98–99
Conscientious objection, 9
Conscription: see Draft
Consent
  as source of power, 65
  withholding of, 68–69, 76,
    107, 115
Conspiracy, charges of, 2
Contempt of court, 2
Conversion, 21
Conviction, strength of, 69,
  101
Cousins, Norman, 12
Critics of nonviolent resis-
  tance, 111–13
Cuba, 112
Czechoslovakia, 63

Daley, Richard, 73n, 76n
Danville, Virginia, 55
Darrow, Clarence, 7
Davis, Angela, 16
Day, Dorothy, 54, 57, 88
Decentralization, 73, 74
Dellinger, David, 11, 111
Deming, Barbara, 54, 56–57
Democracy
  of group nonviolent resis-
    tance, 100–101
  and nonviolent resistance,
    105–108
Democratic convention of
  1964, 16
Deutsch, Karl, 66
Direct action, 22–23
Discipline, necessity for, 57
Disruption, resistance as, 77
Dodd, Thomas, 12
Dominance, 110
Dominican Republic, 63
Draft, military, 9, 95, 111
Dukhobors, 22

Economic boycott, 15
Einstein, Albert, 50
Eisenhower, Dwight, 11
Elite, the
  character of, 72
  functionaries of, 72
  relation to the mass, 103
Emigration
  as nonconsent, 107
  as social noncooperation, 77
Empathy, 49; see also Sympathy and role-playing, 50
Ends and means, 39–40, 53

Ethics, of individual vs. group
  nonviolence, 102
Expression, as parameter of resistance, 108–109

Fallibility, human, conse-
  quences of, 86
Fanon, Franz, 112
Farmer, James, 13, 81, 81n
Fasting, 56
Fellowship of Reconciliation
  (FOR), 8n, 12, 13
Festinger, Leon, 45
Field, G. C., 112
Ford, Henry, 8
Ford Co., 11
Fortas, Abe, 117
Fox, Joan, 49n
Frank, Jerome, 58, 109
Freedom Rides, 13
Freud, Sigmund, 58
Friends, Society of, 42, 52, 59;
  see also American Friends
  Service Committee
  participation among, 106
  plain speaking of, 111
Functionaries of the elite, 72

Galtung, Johan, 108, 109
Games, 113n
Gamson, William A., 66n
Gandhi, Mohandas, 39, 52, 59,
  80n, 94
  democracy of, 107
  example of, 11
  on human beings as fallible,
    86n
  as leader, 71, 84
  multiple goals of, 110
  openness of, 111
  sources of, 6
Garrison, William Lloyd, 5–6
Ghana, 64, 92
Goals, expressive and instrumental, 108–109
Goffman, Erving, 42
Golden Rule, 1
Greece, 73–74
Green, T. H., 66
Greensboro, North Carolina,
  14–15
Gregg, Richard, 45, 95
  as analyst of nonviolence,
    18, 40, 42, 43
  on expression, 108
  on group vs. individual ac-
    tion, 52
  on human unity, 36–37
  on substitutes for war, 53
Griffin, Georgia, 55
Group for the Advancement of
  Psychiatry (GAP), 58
Group nonviolent resistance,
  33, 60–84, 114; see also In-
  dividual nonviolent resis-
  tance

assumptions of, 60–64
components of, 68–71
example of, 79–81
in foreign affairs, 82–84
hierarchy and, 71–76
vs. individual, 60, 63, 100–
  102
power and consent, 64–67
safety of, 82
techniques of. 76–79
Guerrilla warfare
  and policy change, 106
  and resistance, 29
  as symbolic violence, 100

Habits, nonviolent, training in,
  42
Hansford, Earle A., 112n
Hitler, Adolf, 39
Hobbes, Thomas, 66
Hoffman, Abbie, 58n
Holmes, John Haynes, 8n
Hopewell, 6
Human unity, and individual
  nonviolent resistance, 38–39,
  41
Hume, David, 66
Humphrey, Hubert, 17

Identification with ruler, 70
Identity, enhanced by conflict,
  61
Immigrants, civil rights of, 7
Incorporation, goal of individual nonviolence, 41
India, 92
Indians, civil rights of, 7
Individual nonviolent resistance, 33, 34–59, 114; see
  also Group nonviolent resistance
  aims of, 38–41
  applications of, 54–58
  assumptions of, 35–38, 63
  contrasted with group ap-
    proach, 81, 100–102
  in mass form, 52–53
  methods of, 46–51
  openness of, 110–111
  power of, 41–44, 64
  questions about, 51–52
  stages of, 45–46
  techniques of, 44
  as tool of elite, 104
Influence, 64
Intensity, weighting for, 106
Intervention, 28
  vs. noncooperation, 78
Irwin, Lord, 66

James, William, 53
Jaspers, Karl, 112
Journal of Conflict Resolution,
  12, 58
Journey of Reconciliation, 13

Jouvenal, Bertrand de, 66

Kellogg-Briand Treaty, 22
Kennan, George, 83n
Kennedy, John F., 16, 55
Kent State University, 73n
Kenya, 64
Kenyatta, Jomo, 64
King, Martin Luther, Jr., 56, 71, 84
  as activist, 18, 51
  failure of in Chicago, 108
  and the Montgomery bus boycott, 92–93
  philosophy of nonviolence, 14, 96–97
King Solomon's Ring, 110
Knowledge, source of power, 42
Kuhn, Manford H., 47n
Ku Klux Klan, 73
Kuper, Leo, 27–28

Labor, rights of, 7
Labor movement, 10–11, 18
Laissez-faire, and group resistance, 100
Lakey, George, 82n
Lasswell, Harold, 66
Law
  enforcement of, as social remedy, 114
  respect for, 89–90
Leadership
  of the masses, 104
  nonviolent, 84
League of Universal Brotherhood, 7
Liberation, 12, 94
Levellers, the, 107
Lewis, John, 111
Lippmann, Walter, 53
Loaves and Fishes, 57
Long Loneliness, The, 57
Lorenz, Konrad, 110
Love, agapic, 86–87
Luthuli, Chief, 108

MacArthur, Douglas, 11
Machiavelli, Niccolo, 66, 103n
MacIver, R. M., 66
MacNamara, Robert, 15
Macon, Georgia, 55
Majority, rule of, 107
Mann, John, 47n
March on Washington, 11, 15–16
Marxists, 111
Mass individual nonviolence, 52–53
Masses, the, 72
  lack of organization of, 73
  relation to the elite, 103
Mayday Tribe, the, 2–3
McLuhan, Marshall, 44
Meditation, in training for nonviolence, 43

Meeker, Robert J., 112n
Mennonites, 7
Merton, Robert, 47
Micro-resistance, 83
Might vs. right, 105
Miller, William, 18, 87, 94
  on a just war, 112
  nonviolent action classified by, 88
Mississippi Freedom Summer, 16
Mitchell, John, 76n
Montgomery, Alabama, 14, 92–93
Morality, and efficacy, 95
Moravians, 4
Morrison, Norman, 49n
Moynihan, Daniel, 117
Muste, A. J., 11, 18
  career of, 10, 95–96
  critic of Walk for Peace, 56
  as pacifist, 8n

Nation, Carrie, 117
National Association for the Advancement of Colored People (NAACP), 13, 16
Nations, use of violence by, 62–63
Negroes with Guns, 111
Neustadt, Richard, 66
New England Non-Resistance Society, 5
New Testament, 6
New York City, 16, 78
Niebuhr, Reinhold, 10–11, 87n, 112
Nieburg, Harold, 106
Nineteenth amendment, 26
Nixon, Richard M., 20n
Nkrumah, Kwame, 64
Noncooperation, 27, 28
  economic, 77–78
  and intervention, 78–79
  political, 78
  social, 77
Nonresistance, 21
Nonviolence, economy of, 61
Nonviolent resistance; see also Combined forms of nonviolent resistance; Group nonviolent resistance; Individual nonviolent resistance
  Christian view of, 85–88
  criticisms of, 111-13
  defined, 21, 22
  efficacy of, 114–16
  kinds of, 11
  problems of, 108–11
  reassessment of, 17–18
  terms used in, 19–25
  theorists vs. activists in, 18
  types of, 25–33
Norway, collective resistance by teachers in, 79–80
Nuclear testing, 1–2

Oakland Black Panthers, 77n
Oaths, refusal of, 78
Obedience, factors in, 70
Obligation, as cause of obedience, 71
One-sided action, limitations of, 13
Oppenheimer, Martin, 82
Optimism, of individual resistance, 102
Order, respect for, 90
Oregon, 7

Pacifists
  changes in, 50
  in Civil War, 7
  exploitation of, 112n
  and nonviolence, 21
  post-Civil War, 7–8
  pre-Civil War, 5
  in World War I, 8–9
Paine, Tom, 117
Palisades Amusement Park, 14
Parks, Rosa, 3
Pascal, Blaise, 117
Passive resistance, 11, 21–22
Peace groups, 12–13
Peace Ship, 8
Peacemakers, 12
Peck, James, 11, 14, 18
Pendle Hill pamphlets, 42
Penn, William, 4
Persuasion
  defined, 21
  and group nonviolence, 64
  tool of nonviolent resistance, 58, 104
Pessimism, of group nonviolence, 102
Philadelphia, Pa., 15
Phillips, Wendell, 7
Philosopher-king, the elite as, 103, 105
Picketing, mass, 10
Plato, 98, 105
Pocahontas, 3, 4
Poverty, inflicted vs. voluntary, 57
Power
  authority as form of, 65
  and consent, 64–67
  demonstration of without violence, 62–63
  by denial of cooperation, 76
  diffusion of, 73
  safety of nonviolent, 82
  sources of, in nonviolence, 42
Power of Nonviolence, The, 40
Pressure, 64
Pritchett, Laurie, 56
Property, destruction of, 111
Protest, 28
  antiwar, 76
  as nonconsent, 76

techniques of, 77–78
visibility of, 77
Psychological study, 36, 37

Quakers, New England, 3; *see
also* Friends, Society of

Randolph, Asa Phillip, 15–16
Rapaport, Anatol, 112*n,* 113*n*
Reagan, Ronald, 73*n*
Reassurance, as phase of non-
violence, 46
*Reflections on Violence,* 112
Religion, and nonviolent resis-
tance, 35; *see also* Christian-
ity
Rent strikes, 16
Resistance, 22, 28, 77
Resolution conflict, as phase of
nonviolence, 46
Respect, basic to nonviolent ac-
tion, 38–41; *see also* Human
unity
Restaurant sit-ins, 14, 48
Revolution, and nonviolent re-
sistance, 90–92
Reward, intermittent, 47*n*
Reynolds, Earle, 2
Right: *see* Might
Ritualization of conflict, 109,
110
Role-playing, 50, 57
Rousseau, Jean-Jacques, 74
Rubin, Jerry, 58*n,* 111
Ruesch, Jurgen, 42
Ruskin, John, 6, 34
Russell, Bertrand, 50
Russia, 63
Rustin, Bayard, 11, 14

SANE, 12
*Saturday Review,* 12
*Satyagraha,* 80*n*
Scale, problem of, 98
Schelling, Thomas, 113*n*
School boycotts, 16
Schwinner, Rosika, 8
Secrecy, 110
Seifert, Harvey, 18, 28
eclectic view of nonviolence,
94–95
Self-fulfilling prophecy, 47, 57
Self-immolation, 48
Self-respect, 59
Self-suffering, 28
Sharp, Gene, 18, 29, 53, 59
on collective resistance, 60*n,*
64, 79–80
on consent, 66
on obedience, 70
organizational scheme of,
30–32
Shridharani, Krishnalal, 80*n*
Shure, Gerald H., 112*n*

Sit-ins
in restaurants, 14, 48
strikes, 11
student, 14–15
Smith, John, 3
Social evolution, and power of
nonviolence, 44
Social structure, as basis for
effective resistance, 72–76
Society, 72
Sociodrama, 93
Solidarity, 69, 71, 73
decentralized, 74
Sorel, George, 112
Sorokin, Pitirim, 40
South Africa, 27, 108
Southern Christian Leadership
Conference (SCLC), 13, 14,
15, 16, 84
St. Louis, Missouri, 14
Stoner's restaurant, 14
Strength, demonstration of,
40–41
Strikes
as economic noncooperation,
77
rent, 16
sit-in, 11
Student Nonviolent Coordinat-
ing Committee (SNCC),
13, 14, 16, 84, 93
internal structure of, 101
Student Peace Union, 12
Students, sit-ins by, 14–15
Suffering, voluntary, 48–50
as communication, 99
and empathy, 49–50
and sympathy, 49
Suffragettes, 9–10
Suggestion, 47, 57
Sympathy, 49

Tactical nonviolent resistance,
88–89
Tactics, use of nonviolence dictated by, 93–94
Taft, William Howard, 8
Tax refusal, 78
Television, 44
Terms used
aggression, 21, 22
civil disobedience, 23–25
direct action, 22–23
nonresistance, 21
nonviolent vs. violent, 19–
21
nonviolent resistance, 21, 22
passive resistance, 21–22
persuasion and conversion,
21
resistance, 22
Third parties, role of, 43–44
Thomas, Norman, 8*n*

Thoreau, Henry David, 24–25,
90
Tocqueville, Alexis de, 107
Tolstoy, Leo, 7, 66, 82
on pacifism, 6
Traffic, disruptions of, 78
Transarmament, 84
Trust, 58, 66*n*
Turn Toward Peace, 12

United Nations, charter of, 22
United States, 63; *see also*
America
Universal Peace Union, 7
Urban League, 13, 16

Vietcong, 83*n*
Vietnam War
and antiwar groups, 12
and civil rights groups, 17
Mayday Tribe on, 2–3
Violence
differing definitions of, 64
drawbacks of, 53
man's belief in efficacy of,
62
provocation of, 27
reaction to, 39
in self-defense, 111
Visibility, 58
*Voyage of the Golden Rule,*
54

Walk for Peace, 55–56
Walker, Charles, 82*n*
War
and group nonviolence, 63–
64
just vs. unjust, 89
substitutes for, 53
War of 1812, 5
War Resisters League, 12
Warren, Josiah, 7
Washington, D.C., 78
Weber, Max, 66, 70
Will, strength of, 69
Williams, Robert, 96, 111–12
Wilson, Dagmar, 12
Wilson, Woodrow, 8
Women, civil rights of, 7, 18
Women Strike for Peace, 12
Women's International League
for Peace and Freedom, 8
Work, basic to nonviolence,
42–43
World community, concept of,
37
World War I, 8–9, 12
World War II, 12
*Wretched of the Earth, The,*
112

Zinn, Howard, 112

1 2 3 4 5 6 7 8 9 10